Log Home Care and Maintenance

Log Home Care and Maintenance

Everything You Need to Know to Buy, Maintain, and Enjoy Your Log Home

Jim Davis

The Lyons Press
Guilford, Connecticut
An imprint of The Globe Pequot Press

The Lyons Press is an imprint of The Globe Pequot Press.

10 9 8 7 6 5 4 3 2 1

Printed in the United States of America

ISBN 1-59228-338-1

Library of Congress Cataloging-in-Publication Data is available on file.

About the Author

Jim Davis started in the log home industry in 1976. After graduating from college with a degree in forestry, he started work drafting floor plans. Moving through the different departments of a log home manufacturer, he gained experience in the different manufacturing processes. In 1995 he took the leap to owning his own manufacturing company. Incorporating his previous experiences in manufacturing, repairing, and restoring log homes, he accepted repair projects as part of the new company. Each year, as that part of the business grew, he devoted more time to researching the many products, techniques, and services available. From home owner contacts and repairing work done by others he realized the need for solid advice on log home maintenance.

Mr. Davis has crewed on or subcontracted for construction and performed repair and restoration work on more than one hundred log homes in twelve states. He also contracts out to home owners who want to perform the work themselves. The author's website is www.logswork.com.

Contents

List of Figures

Preface

This book was written for those of us who love log products, want to maintain their appearance, and would like to prolong their appeal. With all the different products and techniques available, the objective is to help the applicator (the person doing the work) understand the dynamics of log work and how to maintain its aesthetic appeal.

Some of the information in this book is readily available through other sources. If you have already conducted some type of research, you have likely discovered that accumulating and collating these resources can be tedious and frustrating. Tedious because one research source requires you to have knowledge that is attained from a dozen other sources. Frustrating because opinions expressed can differ from one source to another or just be unreliable. Unfortunately, you don't find that out until after the work is done. I hope my education, experience, and reliable sources I have found make this process easier for you.

We start with wood properties and chemistry so you can develop a basic understanding of the dynamics of log products. You also will read about why it is important to maintain these products and what their enemies are. Following this is inspection of the log structure and why the different points are important. You will then move on to a "how-to" section on cleaning, preserving, staining, and sealing your log products. This section also lists the equipment and tools you will need. We even have charts, graphs, and discussions on different products in the marketplace, so you can compare and choose the type of products best suited for your application. You will not find any product recommendations in this book. Although I have my preferences, there are few specific products that are the best for every application. In other words, what works well in Vermont does not necessarily work well in New Mexico. If you are like me, you don't like listening to claims of "our products are the best."

You will then read about common log problems, their causes, and how to fix them. I finish with references to sources that I believe provide reliable information.

Introduction

Why Do This Book?

I had just graduated from college with a degree in forestry in 1976. I loved wood. I wanted to be around wood. Being a hands-on person, I wasn't sure where that was going to lead me. The job market wasn't looking promising. A local sawmill was hiring, so was the local reel maker. I wasn't sure I was up for working in a factory. One day I noticed an ad placed by a log home manufacturer. They were looking for a drafter—someone to draw floor plans. I had some experience drafting for my father, who was an engineer, so I applied. The owner called and invited me to the plant. As soon as I arrived, I knew this was where I wanted to be. During the interview, the owner told me he could afford to pay me only $3.25 an hour. I had no idea how much a drafter should make, but I didn't really care. I took the job. It wasn't long before I was making cut sheets, laying out log walls, and preparing shipping documents.

Now, here I am twenty-six years later. I am writing about what I have learned. I have seen good companies and bad companies. I have heard some good advice, and some bad advice. I have found my share of good people to listen to, and far more people to not pay attention to. I have been involved in just about every facet of log home manufacturing, building, and restoring. Consequently, what really upsets me is driving past a log home that has fallen into disrepair.

The reason for this is simple: neglect. Neglect comes from misunderstanding or being misled or just plain idleness. I cannot recount the number of times I have looked at a job and found that with some preventive maintenance, bigger problems could have been avoided.

I will attempt to provide you with a good working knowledge of some of the common problems, how to avoid them, and how to fix them.

This book is not about the best log product, cleaner, preservative, stain, caulk, or chink. There is no single best product. Because methods and materials are constantly undergoing revisions, I will not recommend any here.

I have built and restored log homes in twelve states. Here's what I have found:

1. Just because the salesperson says so, doesn't necessarily make it so.
2. The same situation in a different environment may call for a different solution.
3. Common sense goes a long way.
4. *Pro*-action is always better than *re*-action.
5. Doing nothing is better than doing something, only when something is wrong.

I started restoring/resealing log homes as a supplement to manufacturing log homes mainly because of the number of calls I received from home owners, builders, and realtors who didn't know what to do or where to begin. When I started in this industry in 1976, restoration/resealing was a nonissue. Resources were few or out of date. Today, we have log home books on design and building (complete with pretty pictures), log home magazines, seminars, research letters, government studies, independent product studies, manufacturer literature, Web sites, and so forth. It almost seems we have an information overload. Everyone is an expert and has the best products!

I did my first few jobs the best I could. But I wasn't satisfied, so I started to research more aggressively. I started with a basic question: "What is the best way to handle this particular situation?" Since the answer usually came in the form of products and methods, I added another question: "What are the best products and methods available?" After hearing many sales pitches and opinions, I also asked: "Who can I trust to give me good information?" Then came the task of putting it all together.

I wrote this book for two reasons. Although I love to restore and reseal log homes, I also understand that there are many log home owners who want to take pride in their ownership by doing some of the maintenance themselves. Why not? It's a good idea. However, they are usually not quite sure where to begin. They have tried to research their problem but have ended up with too many contradictory views, or the research became so deep, they got lost in the details.

I also think that some of the work done by others would have been better if the information they'd received up front was sound.

What This Book Is

This book is mainly a compilation of resources, sprinkled with my personal observations and experiences. If you see something in this book you think you have seen before, you probably have. By referring to and quoting from resources I believe are reliable, I want to provide you with something you can use either as a starting point for your research, or to fill in with the information you need to tackle your project. My sincere hope is that this book points you in the direction of finding your answers, without encountering too many contradictory opinions along the way.

To illustrate this point, here's one of my favorite stories about a log home show I attended. I was visiting with all the manufacturers and independent contractors, asking questions. At the first booth I stopped at I wanted to make sure I was asking all the pertinent questions. I also wanted to assess how complete and accurate the answers I got were. Then I moved on to the next booth. I asked the same questions, but the answers were a little different. "Our products are better because . . . our methods are better because . . ." By the end of the day, my head was swimming with all the information I had gathered. I was now trying to remember who said what and why.

Well, I guess I'm a slow learner because I keep going there. That's why this is not a "send me more information and I will send you a quote" book. This book is designed to be a "how-to" manual and a valuable resource for the home owner or the professional.

So here's a suggestion: Scan through this book first. Get a feel for where everything is. Use a Post-it to mark the pages and sections you want to come back to. Then read the first chapter, paying particular attention to the wood chemistry, log shrinkage, and moisture sections. From there, move to the chapter or section that suits your situation. References are made to other sections for more complete reading.

Why Is Maintenance Important?

Like any other investment, if you don't take care of your log home, it will fail. Because of the mass of logs, a problem may take some time to show, but, without maintenance, the logs will eventually fail.

Log home owners today like the look of the new structure and want to keep it that way. While that can be achieved to some degree, reality has to become a part of the picture. Even if the home owner wants the logs to age to a dark brown or gray patina, certain measures have to be taken to protect and seal the log components.

We have all heard the stories of 3,000-year-old log structures. We may have seen pictures of some of them and think all log structures can last this long. The common perception is that log homes will last for centuries. Compared to stick homes that last fifty to one hundred years, there is quite an incentive to build a log home with the intention of passing it down to our children and our children's children. That is quite a legacy. After all, who wouldn't like to say at a dinner party that "we're going to spend some time at our log home up by the mountain lake." Oh the visions that statement conjures up! A woodland setting, a stone fireplace, a fly rod by the door, lazy mornings and romantic nights. In a fast-paced world, we all dream of that.

Then you hear of the log homes with rotted logs and leaky windows. Owners who can't get rid of the draft, and doors that stick. Suddenly you think that maybe a log home is not a good idea. But log homes can be a good idea. You just have to understand that like everything else, they need to be maintained. You have to periodically check the sealant and stain to make sure they are still doing the job they were intended to do. You have to identify any problems and find out how to correct them. We will discuss some of the common problems and their solutions. Because of the changing nature of sealants and stains, we will also discuss some of the popular ones today and look at where they seem to be going in the future.

By properly maintaining your log home, you are effectively combating the three main enemies:

1. sun
2. moisture
3. insects

Based on my experience, I generally add a fourth:

4. neglect

(1) *Sun.* The most common problem experienced by log home owners is a condition called *weathering*. Weathering starts almost immediately on untreated, exposed wood. This process is the breaking down of the wood fibers and the destruction of cellulose. Generally, it affects only the wood at or near the surface of the log, but over time it can go deeper. By itself, weathering is not considered a serious problem. But weathering opens up many cracks, allowing for moisture, rot, and insects to set in. At higher elevations, the sun's UV rays may cause more severe weathering, with logs turning gray. Not only

do most home owners like the look of new logs, but, as you will find out later, weathered logs are a sign that the decaying process has already started. (See the section on "Weathering" in Chapter 5 for more information.)

(2) Moisture. Moisture damage is most commonly caused by prolonged exposure to rain or snow, particularly if the wood has not had the opportunity to completely dry out in between exposures. Wood is an amazingly resilient material and will retain most of its qualities if it is maintained. For thermal efficiency, fire safety, and structural integrity altogether, logs have no equal. But, allowed to decay, they will lose those properties and invite a whole host of other problems. For instance, the spores from fungal growths can affect those with allergies. Also, wet, decaying logs invite insect infestations. (See the section on "Rot and Decay" in Chapter 5 for more information.)

(3) Insects. As a general rule, wood-boring insects do not like dead, dry wood. Wet wood, however, becomes a lair to lay their eggs and form colonies. Once infested, it can become quite an expensive chore getting rid of them. The best defense is to keep the logs dry, close up any entry holes, and destroy any insect routes into the house. (See the section on "Insect Damage" in Chapter 5 for more information.)

(4) Neglect. I place neglect on three different levels. The first level is using inappropriate products and not following up on their effectiveness. The next level is hiding the problem; out of sight, out of mind. The final level is procrastination, or doing nothing. I consider these to all be the result of a lack of reliable information. By understanding the need to regularly perform maintenance functions, home owners not only reduce the occurrence of problems caused by weathering, rot and decay, and insects, but also achieve peace of mind and satisfaction with their decision to purchase a log home.

A Brief History

As the saying goes, *before we can know where we are going, we have to know where we have been.* We will begin our history in the late 1960s and early 1970s. The majority of log homes were cabins or vacation getaways that were most likely produced by the local sawmill. You could count on one hand the number of dedicated manufacturers who had conducted some kind of engineering study for their products and produced them using specialized equipment. The industry was too small for the caulking and stain manufacturers to devote any real resources to developing appropriate sealing materials. These materials worked okay, but they did not have a long service life. Sealants, or caulks and chinks, generally had an effective service life of five to ten years. Finishes, or more precisely stains, had a shorter effective life span, usually one to two years. But these materials were light-years ahead of the mortar mixes and other daubing materials traditionally used. Because of them, log home sales enjoyed steady increases for a few years.

Another reason for the appeal of log homes came from the sales pitch that they needed "little or no maintenance." At that time, most research sources did not focus on the combined dynamics of log structures. The biggest studies conducted during this time were for energy efficiency and fire safety. These were conducted not only to energize sales, but to deal with the banking and insurance industries' reluctance to finance and insure log homes. After all, their main impression of a log home owner was that of some backwood, do-it-yourselfer wanting cheap housing. Complete with dirt floors, bugs, and wood-fired cookstoves! Then the recession of the late 1970s hit, and log homes became a commodity few could enjoy. Retrenchment was the issue. Having been through the ups and downs of the industry before, some companies looked for ways to even out their production schedules and make their products better. Better equipment was installed, an industry association was formed, and manufacturers started working with one another to improve the industry as a whole.

The next renaissance happened in the late 1980s, and it pretty much continues today. During this period, the larger more established manufacturers were able to conduct research into methods that would improve their products. The industry was reaching a critical mass where caulking, chinking, and stain manufacturers saw the serious need for reliable, long-term products. No longer were the manufacturers relying on outdated information relating to log homes. In addition to research already available through the USDA Forest Products Laboratory, chemists, biologists, universities, and other companies wanting to sell to the industry were chipping in and providing much needed research. Sealing products were being developed specifically for the log home industry. Silicone and butyl rubber caulks were now being replaced by siliconized acrylic latex caulks, stains had more UV protecting solids, and the consumer was inundated with whose products were better. Educating the consumer went from individual research to weekend workshops and home shows. More magazines appeared on the scene offering educational articles. Books on log homebuilding appeared in bookstores.

With the advent of the computer and the World Wide Web, consumers now have more resources than ever available to educate themselves. However, I believe that the good resources are too scattered and need to be consolidated for easier use. My objective is to "link up" these resources and provide accurate information in a "go to" handbook.

Log Home Care
and
Maintenance

Chapter 1

Wood Chemistry and Moisture

Wood Chemistry

To fully appreciate the reasons for maintaining your log home, let's take a quick look at the chemistry of logs. The vast majority of log homes are made out of softwoods (such as pine, spruce, and fir). While most of these principles can be adapted to hardwoods, we will focus our discussion on softwoods. (See Figure 1–1.)

Wood Cells

The structural elements of wood are the *wood cells*. They are of various sizes and shapes and are firmly cemented together. These cells are also called *wood fibers* or *tracheids*. These fibers run longitudinally. Additionally, some cells are oriented from the center of the tree (the pith) toward the bark. These are called *rays*. Now, a wood cell is a cavity surrounded by a rigid wall. The wall is comprised mainly of *cellulose, lignin, and hemicellulose. Green* wood is defined as wood in which the cell walls are saturated with water. However, green wood usually contains additional water in the cell cavity. When wood cells have reached a moisture content where the cell walls are saturated but no water exists in the cell cavity, the *fiber saturation point* has been reached. For our purposes, the fiber saturation point of wood averages about 30 percent moisture content. In practice though, there are different methods used to measure the fiber saturation point of various woods with results varying from 27 percent to 35 percent. Fiber saturation point is discussed in more detail later under "Log Shrinkage" because it is an important point to understand *why* logs do not shrink appreciably as they are drying until they have reached the fiber saturation point.

Bark

As part of a living plant, the bark serves a purpose much like human skin. It is the primary defense shield for the mechanics going on inside. It shields the cambium layer and sapwood against the harmful UV rays from sunlight, excessive moisture from rain, and the destruction

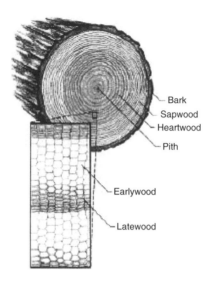

Figure 1–1. Cross section of a typical log.
Reprinted: *Water Repellents and Water Repellent Preservatives for Wood,* Williams, R. Sam, U.S. Dept. of Agriculture, Forest Service, Forest Products Laboratory, FPL-GTR-109

of wood-boring insects. Just like skin, it is not ironclad and can be damaged. Depending on the nature of the damage, the tree will attempt to heal the wound. When it is successful, the bark forms a scar. As a result, the soundness of the wood underneath can only be measured once the tree is harvested. When it is not successful, the bark allows sunlight, moisture, and insects to infect the wood. The process of decay and rot then can start. Even though trees are our only renewable resource, trees with these defects are still harvested and milled to remove as many of these defects as possible.

Sapwood

A tree grows by cells dividing at the cambium layer. This is a thin layer of living cells found just under the bark. As the tree grows, sapwood is created in the form of *annual growth rings*. These growth rings are divided into two parts: *earlywood* and *latewood*. The wider, lighter colored band between growth rings is the earlywood and the thinner, denser band is the latewood. As the tree gets older, sapwood transforms into heartwood through a chemical process.

Sapwood is located between the bark and the heartwood. The distinction between sapwood and heartwood is normally the lighter color of the sapwood band. Its primary job is the storage of protein and nutrients needed by the tree. It also serves as the conductor of water or sap up and down the trunk. A characteristic of the entire cross section of wood, but more pronounced in the sapwood band, is the growth pattern of the annual rings. Forest-stand dynamics determine the growth patterns of trees. Soil conditions, condition of undergrowth, access to sunlight, and competing tree species are examples of forest-stand dynamics. Due to the nature of growth patterns, reaction wood is formed in the sapwood layer. Reaction wood is the primary cause of the warping, bowing, and twisting characteristics found in end-use wood products. Finally, sapwood by itself is not resistant to decay.

Heartwood

The innermost component of a log is the heartwood. Heartwood is made up of mostly inactive cells. These cells no longer store food or act as a channel for water or sap. As a tree grows and sapwood transforms into heartwood, an extractive process takes place. These extractives are the primary reason for the level of resistance to decay a particular tree has. Extractives also increase the stability of the log by reducing the ability of moisture to be absorbed and desorbed into the heartwood band. It becomes harder for moisture to get in or out of this layer.

As a general rule, faster-growing trees have more sapwood than heartwood. In fact, because of research conducted over the years to improve growth cycles and conditions, most of the trees harvested today have this characteristic. Due mainly to a higher level of humidity and supply of moisture, older-growth stands found on the West Coast, which are mainly cedars, firs, and redwoods, do not require a large sapwood band and thus develop wider bands of heartwood. It is this characteristic and the higher concentration of extractives that lends these trees the ability to be more resistant to decay and rot.

For our purposes, the most important feature of wood chemistry occurs at the time of harvesting. When a tree is harvested, the natural defenses have to be replaced by man-made products. The bark and cambium layer have to be completely removed so that the new products can do their job. Some people think it is pretty to leave some of the bark or cambium layer on. While the aesthetic appeal of this treatment may attract some owners, that is about the only benefit there is. Because the bark will hold in moisture and the cambium layer is a food source, you might as well fill out an invitation for an invasion of insects and decay organisms.

The other reason for removing the bark is to allow the log to dry to the *equilibrium moisture content*. (See Figure 1–2.) At this level, a dry, sound log will not decay. As stated before, most of the trees harvested today are faster growing and as a result have more sapwood. Because one of sapwood's primary functions is the storage of water, it is not uncommon to find a moisture content as high as 250 percent. While a log

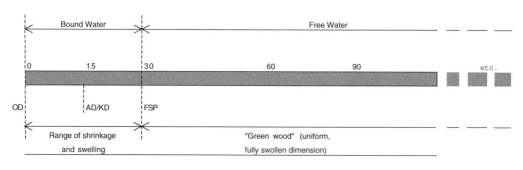

OD= Oven-dry
AD= Typical value of seasoned air dried logs (~14%)
KD= Typical value of kiln dried logs (~14%)
FSP= Fiber Saturation Point (~30%)

Source: *Understanding Wood - A Craftsman's Guide to Wood Technology,*
Hoadley R. Bruce, Taunton Press, copyright 2000

Figure 1–2. Depiction of moisture content values.

dries down to a moisture content of about 30 percent (the *fiber satura-tion point*), appreciable shrinkage is not experienced. Drying from the fiber saturation point down to the equilibrium moisture content, how-ever, the log will experience significant shrinkage. At 30 percent mois-ture content and lower, a log will release the stresses and reveal the tendencies it developed as it grew (reaction wood). Some of those ten-dencies include warping, cupping, bowing, and twisting. These ten-dencies will also aggravate checking and cracking.

Log Shrinkage

There are two types of water found in a live tree, *free water* and *bound water*. As stated before, prior to being harvested, the moisture content of most live softwoods used in log home construction can range from 100 percent to about 250 percent. Moisture accumulates mainly in the cell cavities. This is the free water. During the drying process, cell cavi-ties lose their moisture before the cell walls do. The point at which the cell cavities have completely lost moisture and all that remains is the moisture in the cell walls is called the *fiber saturation point*. For most common softwoods, this point is usually around 30 percent. At the fiber saturation point in the drying process, the logs have not changed dimensionally. The wood cells will maintain their shape so long as the cell walls are fully saturated. The water in the cell walls is the bound water. Once below the fiber saturation point, more dramatic dimensional and other changes begin to occur. To reach the *equilibrium moisture content*, the water in the cell walls will begin to evaporate. As the log continues to dry toward the equilibrium moisture content, the evaporation of the bound water causes the most dimensional changes. As you can see on the log profile diagram (see Figure 1–3), there are three faces that concern us pertaining to shrinkage. *Tangential, radial,* and *longitudinal* or *length*. Under most circumstances, longitudinal shrinkage is negligible, generally 0.2 percent or less. In the field, we disregard this measure. The tangential and radial faces, however, experience a much higher percentage change as bound water evaporates. These changes can be seen in Figure 1–4, which shows the approximate shrinkage for the most common species used in log home construction. Also occurring during this phase is the release of stresses brought on by growth patterns the tree developed while alive, and the stresses released due to drying.

In a perfect world, every tree would get the same amount of sunlight and moisture and grow on level ground. But in the real world, we see the stresses of growth patterns when logs twist, bow, warp, cup, crack, and check. Have you ever stayed in a log home, recently built out of "green" timbers? You might hear an occasional popping sound. Sometimes, these sound like a gun going off. To the uninitiated, you

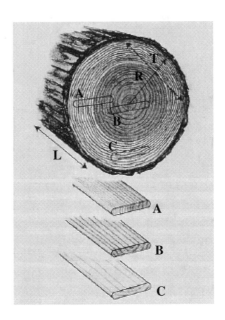

Figure 1–3. Log profile diagram.
Lumbar grain affects finish performance: (a) edge-grain (vertical-grain or quartersawn) board; (b) edge-grain board containing pith; (c) flat-grain (slash-grain or plainsawn) board. Arrows show radial (R), tangential (T), and longitudinal (L) orientation of wood grain. Reprinted: *Water Repellants and Water Repellant Preservatives for Wood,* Williams, R. Sam, U.S. Dept. of Agriculture, Forest Service, Forest Products Laboratory, FPL-GTR-109.

Hardwoods	Tangential	Radial	T/R	Softwoods	Tangential	Radial	T/R
Ash, Black	7.8	5.0	1.7	Bald cypress	6.2	3.8	1.6
Ash, White	7.8	4.9	1.6	Cedar, Alaska	6.0	2.8	2.1
Birch, White	8.6	6.3	1.4	Cedar, Western Red	5.0	2.4	2.1
Birch, Yellow	9.2	7.2	1.3	Douglas Fir (coastal)	7.8	5.0	1.6
Cherry, Black	7.1	3.7	1.9	Douglas Fir (inland)	7.6	4.1	1.9
Maple, Red	8.2	4.0	2.0	Fir, Balsam	6.9	2.9	2.4
Maple, Sugar	9.9	4.8	2.1	Pine, Eastern White	6.1	2.1	2.9
Oak, Black	11.1	4.4	2.5	Pine, Loblolly	7.4	4.8	1.5
Oak, Live	9.5	6.6	1.4	Pine, Lodgepole	6.7	4.3	1.6
Oak, Northern Red	8.6	4.0	2.2	Pine, Ponderosa	6.2	3.9	1.6
Oak, Southern Red	11.3	4.7	2.4	Pine, Western White	7.4	4.1	1.8
Oak, White	10.5	5.6	1.8	Spruce, Engelmann	7.1	3.8	2.1
Walnut, Black	7.8	5.5	1.4	Spruce, Red	7.8	3.8	2.1

Source: *Understanding Wood - A Craftsman's Guide to Wood Technology*, Hoadley R. Bruce, Taunton Press, copyright 2000

Figure 1–4. Approximate shrinkage as a percent of green dimension, from green to oven-dry moisture content.

might think your home is beginning to fall down. In reality, the logs are acclimating to the equilibrium moisture content.

To reach equilibrium, the average log will dry to a moisture content of 6 to 11 percent. Because most log products are shipped with a moisture content around 20 percent, they are considered "green" and will experience additional shrinkage. As we said before, the dimensional changes experienced as logs dry below the fiber saturation point are more pronounced along the tangential and radial faces. To illustrate the point, let's look at an example.

Species – *Lodgepole Pine*   MC – *25%*
log size – *~ 10" wall height – 8'0"*
EMC – *11%*

With all other factors being equal, the question is, *how much additional shrinkage will the wall logs experience before reaching the equilibrium moisture content?*

According to our chart, a log from a lodgepole pine will lose 4.3 percent radially and 6.7 percent tangentially from the fiber saturation point to oven-dry moisture content. For our purposes, oven-dry moisture content is unobtainable. Let's say that to reach the equilibrium moisture content, the logs will lose half those values. In an 8-foot high wall with logs laid horizontally, there will be ten courses of logs. Each course will lose between a quarter-inch and almost a half-inch. Over ten courses, that adds up to $2\frac{1}{2}$ inches to 5 inches of height lost to additional drying. If there are any posts used in the structure, assuming the same moisture conditions, shrinkage in these posts would be only 1 percent or a quarter of an inch. Without slip joints, settling plates, and settling gaps, a home built with green logs will soon be out of plumb, level, and square. Windows and doors stick, extensive sealant failures become commonplace, and, in extreme cases, structural failures may occur. Your dream home becomes a nightmare and remediation becomes expensive. (See Figure 1–5.)

Equilibrium Moisture Content

Before we begin, the term *equilibrium moisture content (EMC)* refers to log material moisture content (MC) and *equilibrium moisture level (EML)* refers to a geographic area's average experienced humidity level.

As the map shows (Figure 1–6.), equilibrium moisture levels vary regionally across this country. Factors affecting these levels include prevailing weather patterns, humidity levels, and temperature. To reach equilibrium moisture content, the base consideration for log

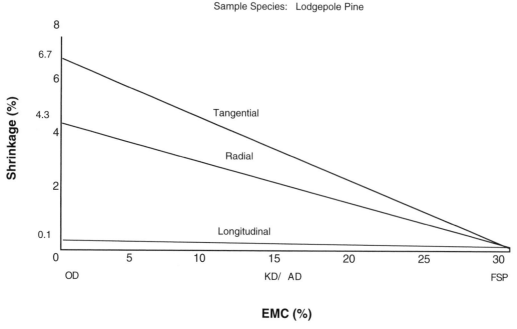

Sample Species: Lodgepole Pine

Figure 1–5. Shrinkage v EMC.

Note: This is a depiction of the percent shrinkage of wood from the Fiber Saturation Point (FSP) to Oven Dry MC (OD). Kiln Dry (KD) and Air Dry (AD) values to reach Equilibrium Moisture Content (EMC) are generally around 15%. It is impossible for log home material to dry to OD moisture content. The majority of seasonal movement will occur between 10% EMC and 20% EMC.

homes is the level of relative humidity as it relates to the equilibrium moisture level. For our purposes, the equilibrium moisture content is the percent of moisture a log will seek so it can acclimate. Once acclimated, seasonal changes in moisture content occur, causing shrinking and swelling of log material. Seasonal changes do not mean a log will go from 8 percent MC to 70 percent MC. EMC levels are averages measured over an extended period of years, not days or weeks. The EMC should not be confused with seasonal changes in moisture content, relative humidity, and log movement.

This topic is discussed in more detail in the next section. You will most likely experience seasonal movement of 1 to 2 percent of the size of your logs. That is why sealants and finishes specific to log homes are designed. They move with the shrinking and swelling of seasonal log movement. The important thing to note here is that shrinking and swelling caused by seasonal movement is a different characteristic of log homes than the EMC process.

For example, your manufacturer ships log material with a moisture content of 20 percent. You find the area you will be building in is in the

Recommended average moisture content for interior wood products in various areas of the United States.
Source: *The Encyclopedia of Wood,* Sterling Publishing Co., 1989 revised edition

Figure 1–6. Average equilibrium moisture levels.

11 percent EML band. This means logs will lose an additional 9 percent moisture content before they acclimate. Based on our log shrinkage chart (Fig. 1–4), assume the logs will shrink approximately 5 percent. For an 8-inch log that would be as much as three-eighths of an inch. By itself, that isn't much. Stacked up horizontally in an 8-foot high wall, total shrinkage will amount to about 4 inches.

The importance of acclimation is first a construction issue, second a maintenance issue. For the purpose of maintenance, milled logs should be assembled as soon as possible, allowing the whole structure to acclimate as one. Also, depending on the moisture content of the delivered logs, the acclimation process can take a couple of weeks or as long as a couple of years. The amount of drying time is determined primarily by the time of year for construction and the equilibrium moisture level. During the summer, drying to EMC is shorter mainly because the EML is higher than in the winter season. (See Figure 1–6.) Again, this is covered in more detail in the following section. If the construction crew does not take log shrinkage into consideration, it will become a major maintenance issue. Failures may occur in the stain application, sealants may bubble and/or suffer adhesion and cohesion failures, windows and doors will stick, rooflines will hump-back, and logs will expose more natural tendencies. This is not a doom and gloom scenario; these problems can be fixed. You just don't want to experience them in your first couple of years.

Moisture, Humidity, and Movement

An important concept to understand at this point is the relationship of moisture, humidity, and log movement. Because this is a book on log home maintenance, we are concerned with this relationship at the point of post construction and settling. This concept is sometimes referred to as *seasonal movement*. Logs constantly shrink and swell due to changes in moisture content brought on by varying weather patterns. This is a fact of life and it will not go away. Our job is to minimize the effects these changes have on our log components by keeping them properly protected and sealed.

Once the logs have reached the equilibrium moisture content, the majority of shrinking has occurred. Now the process of seasonal movement takes over. Seasonal movement is a reaction of wood based on its moisture content to weather conditions, the most prominent being *relative humidity* (RH).

Moisture content is the ratio of the weight of water in wood to the weight of the wood when it is completely dry. Completely dry wood is often referred to as oven-dry wood. In the world of log homes, there is no such thing as oven-dry wood. As stated earlier, all log materials will have some degree of moisture present, usually between 6 percent and 11 percent. That is the equilibrium moisture content.

Humidity is a term referring to moisture vapor in the atmosphere. There are two types of humidity: absolute and relative. Because humidity levels depend on temperature, relative humidity is a ratio of actual moisture in the atmosphere at a given temperature to the most the atmosphere can hold at the same temperature, the absolute humidity. This is expressed as a percentage. The important fact to remember here is that relative humidity is the primary source of shrinking and swelling in house logs.

As the percent level of humidity rises, the saturation point of the atmosphere is being reached, called the *dew point*. The dew point is the temperature at which the atmosphere can no longer hold more moisture. This is all well and good, but we are not meteorologists. What does this have to do with log movement? Most of us associate moisture with rain and snow. But humidity plays a bigger role in the seasonal movement of logs.

When temperatures rise in the summer, the atmosphere has the ability to hold more moisture, just as when temperatures dip in the winter, the atmosphere can hold less. High temperatures with high humidity means logs swell; conversely, low temperatures with low humidity means logs shrink. If we experienced low humidity of say 20 percent in the winter and high humidity of 80 percent in the summer, we would see the moisture content of logs go from 6 percent to 15 percent. The difference of 9 percent is a third of our shrinkage value, which could approximate out to one-quarter of an inch. Total movement of a quarter-inch is not normally a structural consideration, but constant swelling and shrinking can test a sealant and the finish's ability to provide long-term, effective coverage. For this reason alone, inexpensive finishes just don't hold up to the energy developed by log homes.

Understanding the concept that logs respond more dramatically than dimension material to changes in environmental conditions is an important step. All wood material moves with changes in moisture content caused by environmental humidity. It doesn't matter if we are talking about log material or dimension material. The sheer mass of logs causes this shrinking and swelling movement to be more dramatic than the wood on your picnic table or even the siding on your house.

The importance of the concept of shrinkage and swelling in log components is graphically displayed between Figures 1–7 and 1–8. In Figure 1–7, just as log material responds to the loss of moisture from the fiber saturation point to the equilibrium moisture content, the material will also respond to changes in relative humidity as depicted in Figure 1–8. Loss of moisture and shrinkage will occur until the log material has reached the EMC for a given area. As depicted in Figure 1–7, that band is usually between 6 percent and 15 percent on the EMC axis. Once that is reached, seasonal fluctuations in relative humidity cause log material to shrink and swell. If, for instance, seasonal relative humidity values fluctuated from 30 percent to 70 percent, EMC would fluctuate between 6 percent and 13 percent. As a result, shrinkage and swelling values would fluctuate between ~2 percent and ~5 percent.

8″ material = 1/8″ – 3/8″
10″ material = 1/4″ – 1/2″
12″ material = 1/4″ – 2/3″

Testing for Moisture Content

The objective is to measure not just the surface MC, but also MC at the heart of the log. Because the surface MC will be lower than at the heart, you will want to know how much more drying your logs will need before they acclimate. I have found the resistance-type moisture meter to

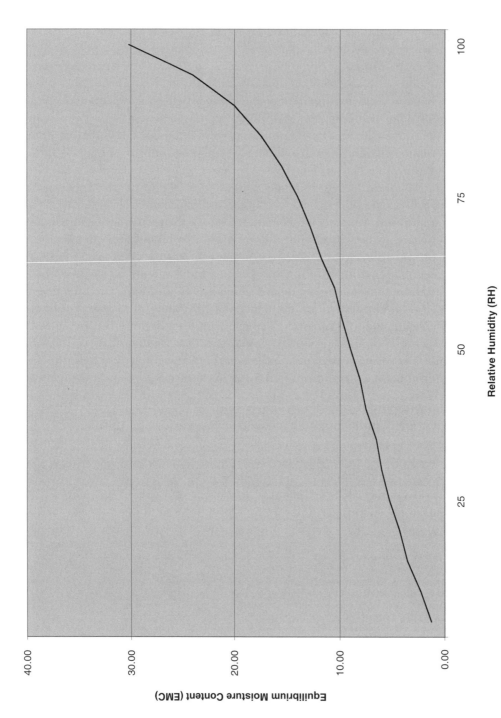

Figure 1–7. EMC to RH, most common woods

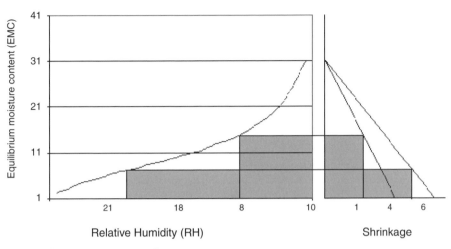

Figure 1–8. Combining Figure 1–7 with Figure 1–5.

work best for this application. The meter itself will have short (about $^1/_4$ to $^1/_2$ inch) pins or electrodes. These meters are readily available in most hardware stores and can test surface MC. The meter should have a receptacle for a hammer probe with longer (about $1^1/_2$ to $2^1/_2$ inches) pins. Depending on availability and the expense of these units, you may try to rent one. The more expensive units have computer chips for species and temperature adjustments. These are valuable features for more extensive usage, such as those discussed in Chapter 5.

Regardless of whether testing MC is done on a delivered log package or on an existing log home, it is not necessary to measure all logs. A representative sampling is the objective. On the face and in the middle of these logs, measure first for surface MC, then heart MC. This is done by driving the electrodes into the log surface. Make a note of each of the readings. Compare readings for each category individually. If your readings show some wide variances, select a few more logs and repeat the process. Average out the readings for surface MC and then the heart MC. Since you are concerned with additional drying, the average heart MC is the more important number. With this number, go back to Figure 1–5 and find the percentage of additional shrinkage most likely to be experienced. Next convert the height of your walls from feet to inches by multiplying the number of feet by twelve. Take the number you have just figured and multiply it by the average heart MC percent. The product is the number of inches you should allow for in additional shrinkage to reach the equilibrium moisture content.

Average Heart MC:	*19%*
Additional Shrinkage:	*~3%*
Wall Height, 8′6″:	*102″*
Anticipated Settling:	*102 × 3% = 3$^1/_4$″*

With regard to the average surface MC readings, these readings are a reference for the application of the finish and sealant. This step in the preparation process will help you achieve the best adhesion of these products.

State	City	Equilibrium moisture content (%)											
		Jan.	Feb.	Mar.	Apr.	May	June	July	Aug.	Sep.	Oct.	Nov.	Dec.
AK	Juneau	16.5	16.0	15.1	13.9	13.6	13.9	15.1	16.5	18.1	18.0	17.7	18.1
AL	Mobile	13.8	13.1	13.3	13.3	13.4	13.3	14.2	14.4	13.9	13.0	13.7	14.0
AZ	Flagstaff	11.8	11.4	10.8	9.3	8.8	7.5	9.7	11.1	10.3	10.1	10.8	11.8
AZ	Phoenix	9.4	8.4	7.9	6.1	5.1	4.6	6.2	6.9	6.9	7.0	8.2	9.5
AR	Little Rock	13.8	13.2	12.8	13.1	13.7	13.1	13.3	13.5	13.9	13.1	13.5	13.9
CA	Fresno	16.4	14.1	12.6	10.6	9.1	8.2	7.8	8.4	9.2	10.3	13.4	16.6
CA	Los Angeles	12.2	13.0	13.8	13.8	14.4	14.8	15.0	15.1	14.5	13.8	12.4	12.1
CO	Denver	10.7	10.5	10.2	9.6	10.2	9.6	9.4	9.6	9.5	9.5	11.0	11.0
DC	Washington	11.8	11.5	11.3	11.1	11.6	11.7	11.7	12.3	12.6	12.5	12.2	12.2
FL	Miami	13.5	13.1	12.8	12.3	12.7	14.0	13.7	14.1	14.5	13.5	13.9	13.4
GA	Atlanta	13.3	12.3	12.0	11.8	12.5	13.0	13.8	14.2	13.9	13.0	12.9	13.2
HI	Honolulu	13.3	12.8	11.9	11.3	10.8	10.6	10.6	10.7	10.8	11.3	12.1	12.9
ID	Boise	15.2	13.5	11.1	10.0	9.7	9.0	7.3	7.3	8.4	10.0	13.3	15.2
IL	Chicago	14.2	13.7	13.4	12.5	12.2	12.4	12.8	13.3	13.3	12.9	14.0	14.9
IN	Indianapolis	15.1	14.6	13.8	12.8	13.0	12.8	13.9	14.5	14.2	13.7	14.8	15.7
IA	Des Moines	14.0	13.9	13.3	12.6	12.4	12.6	13.1	13.4	13.7	12.7	13.9	14.9
KS	Wichita	13.8	13.4	12.4	12.4	13.2	12.5	11.5	11.8	12.6	12.4	13.2	13.9
KY	Louisville	13.7	13.3	12.6	12.0	12.8	13.0	13.3	13.7	14.1	13.3	13.5	13.9
LA	New Orleans	14.9	14.3	14.0	14.2	14.1	14.6	15.2	15.3	14.8	14.0	14.2	15.0
ME	Portland	13.1	12.7	12.7	12.1	12.6	13.0	13.0	13.4	13.9	13.8	14.0	13.5
MA	Boston	11.8	11.6	11.9	11.7	12.2	12.1	11.9	12.5	13.1	12.8	12.6	12.2
MI	Detroit	14.7	14.1	13.5	12.6	12.3	12.3	12.6	13.3	13.7	13.5	14.4	15.1
MN	Minneapolis-St. Paul	13.7	13.6	13.3	12.0	11.9	12.3	12.5	13.2	13.8	13.3	14.3	14.6
MS	Jackson	15.1	14.4	13.7	13.8	14.1	13.9	14.6	14.6	14.6	14.1	14.3	14.9
MO	St. Louis	14.5	14.1	13.2	12.4	12.8	12.6	12.9	13.3	13.7	13.1	14.0	14.9
MT	Missoula	16.7	15.1	12.8	11.4	11.6	11.7	10.1	9.8	11.3	12.9	16.2	17.6
NE	Omaha	14.0	13.8	13.0	12.1	12.6	12.9	13.3	13.8	14.0	13.0	13.9	14.8
NV	Las Vegas	8.5	7.7	7.0	5.5	5.0	4.0	4.5	5.2	5.3	5.9	7.2	8.4
NV	Reno	12.3	10.7	9.7	8.8	8.8	8.2	7.7	7.9	8.4	9.4	10.9	12.3
NM	Albuquerque	10.4	9.3	8.0	6.9	6.8	6.4	8.0	8.9	8.7	8.6	9.6	10.7
NY	New York	12.2	11.9	11.5	11.0	11.5	11.8	11.8	12.4	12.6	12.3	12.5	12.3
NC	Raleigh	12.8	12.1	12.2	11.7	13.1	13.4	13.8	14.5	14.5	13.7	12.9	12.8
ND	Fargo	14.2	14.6	15.2	12.9	11.9	12.9	13.2	13.2	13.7	13.5	15.2	15.2
OH	Cleveland	14.6	14.2	13.7	12.6	12.7	12.7	12.8	13.7	13.8	13.3	13.8	14.6
OK	Oklahoma City	13.2	12.9	12.2	12.1	13.4	13.1	11.7	11.8	12.9	12.3	12.8	13.2
OR	Pendleton	15.8	14.0	11.6	10.6	9.9	9.1	7.4	7.7	8.8	11.0	14.6	16.5
OR	Portland	16.5	15.3	14.2	13.5	13.1	12.4	11.7	11.9	12.6	15.0	16.8	17.4
PA	Philadelphia	12.6	11.9	11.7	11.2	11.8	11.9	12.1	12.4	13.0	13.0	12.7	12.7
SC	Charleston	13.3	12.6	12.5	12.4	12.8	13.5	14.1	14.6	14.5	13.7	13.2	13.2
SD	Sioux Falls	14.2	14.6	14.2	12.9	12.6	12.8	12.6	13.3	13.6	13.0	14.6	15.3
TN	Memphis	13.8	13.1	12.4	12.2	12.7	12.8	13.0	13.1	13.2	12.5	12.9	13.6
TX	Dallas-Ft. Worth	13.6	13.1	12.9	13.2	13.9	13.0	11.6	11.7	12.9	12.8	13.1	13.5
TX	El Paso	9.6	8.2	7.0	5.8	6.1	6.3	8.3	9.1	9.3	8.8	9.0	9.8
UT	Salt Lake City	14.6	13.2	11.1	10.0	9.4	8.2	7.1	7.4	8.5	10.3	12.8	14.9
VA	Richmond	13.2	12.5	12.0	11.3	12.1	12.4	13.0	13.7	13.8	13.5	12.8	13.0
WA	Seattle-Tacoma	15.6	14.6	15.4	13.7	13.0	12.7	12.2	12.5	13.5	15.3	16.3	16.5
WI	Madison	14.5	14.3	14.1	12.8	12.5	12.8	13.4	14.4	14.9	14.1	15.2	15.7
WV	Charleston	13.7	13.0	12.1	11.4	12.5	13.3	14.1	14.3	14.0	13.6	13.0	13.5
WY	Cheynne	10.2	10.4	10.7	10.4	10.8	10.5	9.9	9.9	9.7	9.7	10.6	10.6

Reprinted: *The Wood Handbook: Wood as an Engineering Material*, U.S. Dept. of Agriculture, Forest Service, Forest Products Laboratory, FPL-GTR-113

Figure 1–9. Equilibrium moisture content of wood, exposed to outdoor atmosphere, in several U.S. locations in 1997.

Chapter 2

Home Design and Inspection

Getting Started

Log home maintenance and restoration is a job best suited for those who can think ahead, prioritize, and work methodically. Establish a baseline and work from there. The baseline is developing a basic knowledge of the log product. That is why it is important to understand *how* wood works before moving on to inspection, initial application, maintenance, and problem solving.

In this chapter we will discuss new construction issues, from designing to log wall erection, as they apply to maintenance issues. We also cover inspecting existing homes. The reason for putting new construction and existing homes together is because most new log home owners want a fresh new appearance. In both cases the starting point is the same. When I receive a call to perform some form of resealing or restoration on an existing home, there are a number of questions that I want answered before I begin. Those questions come later in the section on "Existing Homes." If the answer calls for stripping the house down to bare wood and removing any existing sealant, the application methods are much like new construction. Where there is a maintenance record and the finish and sealant can be established, move on to Chapter 4, Regular Maintenance. If there are problems with the structure, incorporate Chapter 5, Log Component Problems with Chapter 6, Log Component Repairs, followed by Chapter 4. All of this is done based on what the home owner wants to accomplish, as well as priorities and budget.

Once the work is done, establish a chart identifying the products used, methods of application, restoration work completed, and future follow-up. With this chart, a conscientious, qualified applicator can perform future regular maintenance functions. If you are conscientious, then this book should help you become qualified.

It is not my intent to discuss which manufacturers are the best or worst, whether you should buy handcrafted or milled, which log home products are the best, or even how to build a log home. It is up to individuals to make up their own minds and decide on what they are comfortable with. My objective is to raise the comfort level on maintenance issues.

I will discuss each subject with maintenance as the focus, and, looking back on my experience, try to think ahead for you. So, as the chapter title states, let's get started.

We will start with new construction at the design phase.

New Construction Design Considerations

Regardless of whether you are using an architect or the company's drafting staff, log home designs today are much more contemporary in their designs. Gone are the days where you could have anything you wanted, as long as it had four walls and a roof. Today, more and more designs are testing the levels of craftsmanship without much regard to how the structure will be maintained. Here, through the eyes of maintenance, are some design points to look for:

Is the overall plan well thought out?

How exposed to the weather is this structure?

Where are the potential trouble spots?

Can they be reached easily?

What kind of equipment is going to be needed for the reapplication of stains and sealants?

Depending on the building site, how often will this have to be done?

Can the home owner do this? Or, is this going to become a nightmare for the applicator?

Are the construction details sufficient to alleviate some of the potential problems?

What is the plan for landscaping?

As you already know, a log home has four main enemies:

1. sun
2. moisture
3. insects
4. neglect

If neglect is not an issue, the dangers from the first three are drastically reduced.

The biggest concern I have about the design stage is planning on how the home is going to be maintained once it is up. Often, accessibility to the entire structure, both high and low, is not built into the design. Maintenance is going to be less expensive and less likely to be put off if the structure is accessible on all sides. Looking at the site plan and elevations, ask yourself:

What equipment is needed to reach all the log components?

Does the applicator need to be a contortionist to reach all components?

Is the estimated cost of regular maintenance acceptable?

Next, are the construction details. Look for potential trouble spots.

Is flashing or a drip edge called for along the entire perimeter of the subfloor?

How far off the ground is the lowest log wall?

Are there any log posts in contact with the ground?

Are the tops of any log deck posts exposed to the weather?

What is called for to seal them?

Is there a sealing system for the exterior log walls? Interior?

How are log butt joints sealed?

Are there any flush butt joints between a vertical member and a horizontal member?

Is the deck or porch floor at the same level as the main floor? Do they step down?

Where will snow accumulate?

How are windows and doors to be set? To the inside? Outside? In the middle?

How will they be trimmed and sealed?

Will the contractor bevel the edge of the bottom log for water runoff?

Are the roof overhangs at least 2 feet on all sides?

Do the plans call for log beams to extend beyond the roofline?

Why are these questions important? Flashing along the perimeter, at the subfloor, provides a deterrent to insect infestation. Having your log walls start at least 18 inches above ground level reduces the problem of "splash back" and the decay organisms that thrive in that environment.

How do you keep a log post from coming in contact with the ground? Outside of raising the concrete pier, you can't. But there is a remedy to the situation. Drill and insert Impel Rods (see Chapter 3).

I went to a log home show recently and overheard the statement by a particular manufacturer's representative that its system did not require any exterior caulking or chinking. My guess is the rep meant to say the home did not need to be caulked, *initially*. While today's production methods may bring us closer to that claim, I do not believe there is a log home or a design that does not or will not require some form of exterior sealant. Claims like that bring back visions of the "low or no maintenance" claims of the 1970s. Do it now or do it later, but your log home will need to be sealed. Period.

Snow and moisture accumulations are most prevalent in corners where porch and/or deck floors attach to the structure. Look for some form of flashing or allowance for drainage at these connections.

One of the largest problem areas in log homes is the installation, trimming, and sealing of windows and doors. The problem areas are usually found at the base of these units, while the cause is from above the units. Water will seep into the logs around the trim, usually through log butt joints or checks and cracks, run down the side of the unit, and start to rot the bottom log. The best solution is to make it a construction issue (see Chapter 3).

By providing some form of shade, roof overhangs and porch roofs shield log components from the harmful UV rays of sunlight. They also allow for water and snow runoff to drop away from the walls so that splash back becomes less of a problem.

You do not want log beams extending beyond the roofline because the wood fibers at the log ends will soak up moisture faster than along the length of the log. Properly sealed, they do not have to be a problem. They just require more attention and maintenance.

If you raise questions about these areas, as they apply to your design, the answers you get should satisfy concerns about sun damage, water damage, and insect damage. That leaves the final question in the design phase: *What kind of maintenance do I need to maintain these protection measures?*

This question is not meant to be a daunting one. You are merely trying to ascertain the extent of extraordinary measures needed to maintain your home and its log components. All of the issues questioned above pertain to most log homes and as such are not extraordinary. By watching for them in the design phase, you are already starting to develop a maintenance inspection list.

Log Delivery and Construction

The next phase for new construction is the log delivery. First and foremost, use common sense. The objective in log home maintenance is to maintain clean, dry, and sound logs. That process starts here.

Are you going to be on-site for the delivery? Did you get a copy of the delivery instructions from the manufacturer? While the manufacturer is the best resource for delivery instructions, some manufacturers leave out some details. Here are some details that have helped me through some successful projects.

When the logs arrive, cover the bundles with sheets of plastic. Put labels on the plastic to identify the bundles. Try to set the bundles down so that access is in the order they will be needed. The main objective is to handle the logs as little as possible and leave them covered for as long as possible.

Next, conduct a quick inventory. Check for missing material and get a feel for where the different materials are. Starter logs, plate logs, gable logs, posts, beams, and so forth. As a bundle inventory is completed, cover the materials back up immediately. Left uncovered, even for a couple of days, you will notice a more distinct discoloration in the uncovered logs versus the covered logs. You may not think this is a

big issue, but, as you will find out in Chapter 5 in the section on "Weathering," the ability of your finish coat to adhere to the logs may be compromised if weathering is allowed to go on for an extended period.

As the walls are being laid up, set up extra stickers (2 × 4s used to keep logs off the ground) on the plastic because sorting through log bundles and moving log materials around is virtually unavoidable. Ground-in dirt and stones are an eyesore, and getting them off a clean log can sometimes be time consuming. Also, when you sort through the bundles, make sure the logs are laid down top up. That way, if you walk on those logs, you are marking a side that will not show. Finally, if you drop a log, and invariably it will happen, clean it immediately.

If the process of laying up log walls is going to take longer than a few days or the weather forecast calls for inclement conditions, have extra sheets of plastic available to cover the walls.

To illustrate that point, on one job site, we were laying up wall logs when the weather called for snow. When we were finished for the day, we covered the walls. By the following morning, the plastic had blown off one of the walls. When we got to the job site, the snow had started to melt and freeze to the top course. We spent an hour just scraping the snow and ice off the course before we could resume laying up wall logs. By keeping the material covered, you will find that not only is weathering more consistent, but working with the material is easier, too.

Closing in the Shell

Now that the logs are laid up, you will probably be anxious to get the roof on and install the windows and doors. As you are doing this, the logs will continue to weather. It will not be noticeable at first, but within two weeks you will see a distinct discoloration difference, especially when you compare the erected logs with an unused log that had been covered during the erection process. Research indicates that bare wood degrades very quickly when exposed to UV light. The USDA Forest Products Laboratory concluded in the November/December 1987 issue of the *Forest Products Journal* (pages 30–31):

Adhesion of both acrylic latex and alkyd oil primer paints to wood signif-icantly reduced after the wood substrate has weathered for 1 or more weeks before painting. These results were observed when evaluating exterior wood finishes in southern Wisconsin. We anticipate a greater effect in warmer and, especially sunnier climates. (emphasis mine)

The same research applies to logs finished with a stain coating. The sooner logs are protected from the elements, the better the applications will adhere to the log surfaces.

Another advantage of applying a finish and sealing the logs at this point is the completeness of coverage, particularly if you are applying the stain with a sprayer. You won't have to worry about overspray on the windows, doors, or trim.

As you progress through the construction phase, think about the possible advantages of applying a finish coat, or preservative, before certain components such as stair stringers, treads, log railings, bal-conies, and so forth are installed. These components will be hard to reach completely after they are installed.

Yes, this will slow the construction process down, but it also low-ers the cost and time involved when you have to do it later. By thinking ahead, with a mind toward maintenance, you are actually saving your-self time and money.

Finally, hard-to-reach components are also usually hard to see. If you need to practice application techniques, these components can be the practice pieces.

Now, let's move on to inspecting existing homes.

Existing Homes

The care for an existing home can be a tricky subject. In this section the assumption is you are considering buying an existing log home or have just bought one. We are also assuming you cannot establish any kind of maintenance record for the structure. A record of maintenance includes:

1. a time frame for the last application of preservatives, coatings, and sealants
2. a description of the materials used
3. a description of other materials previously used
4. restoration or repairs completed

Without some form of record, it is impossible to establish whether new materials are compatible with the old materials. Compatibility is a big issue today because product chemistries and warranties depend on it. Without that record, stripping the log components back down to bare wood is usually the only option. A record of maintenance does not mean log components won't have to be stripped, it just means a starting point—a baseline—has been established.

With a maintenance record, move on to the next step—the home's history. This is established by the following list of questions.

1. Who manufactured the log package?
2. What is the log species?
3. Are there any additions added to the initial structure?
4. What were the materials used in previous applications?
5. Who built the structure?
6. How old is the structure?
7. Are there any existing problem areas? Obvious rot, decay, or insect infestations? Coating and or sealant failures? Air/weather infiltration?
8. Are there any imminent problem areas?
9. What do you want the structure to look like when you are done?
10. What kind of budget are you working with?
11. Do you have a priority list?

Although an "I don't know" answer to any or all of these questions doesn't stop the process, more information is always better.

If the manufacturer can be determined, production methods, wood species, and anything that may apply to maintaining the structure can be established. A phone call to the manufacturer may speed up the rest of the process. By knowing who the builder is, you can get a better feel for the quality of the construction. The age of the structure also gives clues to other maintenance issues and potential problems. Materials used during the last maintenance would give you some idea of what shape the house is in. They would also raise any compatibility issues that need to be dealt with and give you some idea of the previous owner's objectives and intentions.

If you are going to attempt maintenance and/or restoration work yourself, answering these questions first will help you organize your work. The other chapters in this manual will help you achieve your goal.

If you plan on contracting with a professional to do this work, be prepared with as many answers to these questions as possible. If the professional does not ask these types of questions, shop elsewhere. The market has grown so much in the last five to ten years that yesterday's methods and products are old news. New products and methods are developed based on current research, and applications require some form of training because warranties have extended periods.

Existing Home Inspection

Buying a new home is a fun experience (at least it should be!). It is usually the largest investment most people make. So who wants to make that type of investment only to find out there is a problem. That is why we have appraisers and home inspection services. However, these professionals are trained and educated to identify problems mainly in stick-frame construction. Although some of them may have "once done a log home," good quality educational services have not been developed for the mainstream inspection services. Marshall & Swift, a large, well-respected source for building cost information, published the *Log Home Appraisal Training Guide* a number of years ago. Unfortunately, its maintenance section covers only one paragraph. Here we are going to look at the log structure and focus on the areas concerning the structural integrity of the log components. We are going to be looking for existing or potential problems. At this point we are only concerned with observations, so make sure to have paper and pencil with you as we go through this survey. At the top of the paper write down these areas of concern:

1. sunlight
2. moisture
3. insects
4. neglect
5. structural

These will remind you of the common problems to look for throughout the inspection process.

Stand back at a point that allows you to see the entire structure. You will want to do this from all sides. Keeping in mind the concerns listed, what is the general appearance of the structure? Is sunlight and moisture weathering one section more than another? How is the current coating holding up? Are your eyes drawn to any feature that looks like a problem? Do the walls look plumb, square, and level? Are there any humps or dips in the roofline? Write down any observations.

Next, move up to the house for a closer inspection. Consider the following, one wall at a time.

Outside Inspection

Site Condition

1. Type of soil?
2. Grade. Away from structure?
3. Vegetation. Distance to log walls?
4. Signs of insects. Mounds? Woodpiles? Swarms?

Foundation/Subfloor Condition

1. Type of foundation. Slab? Crawl space? Full basement?
2. Material. Block? Poured concrete? Signs of cracks?
3. Sill seal?
4. Subfloor facing. Condition? Secured to foundation?

Log Wall Condition

1. Overall appearance. Plumb? Bows? Secured to foundation?
2. Distance from ground.
3. Sill flashing.
4. Log texture. Rough? Smooth?
5. Are logs browning or grayed from weather?
6. Obvious areas of decay? Wet logs? Soft or punky logs? Signs of patching? Material?
7. Obvious signs of weather infiltration?
8. Corner log appearance. Solid? Plumb? Checking? Decay?
9. Aggressive log checking?
10. Caulk/chink appearance. Adhesion to logs? Material breaking down? Not accepting stain? Chalking? Brittle?
11. Stain/finish appearance. Bubbling? Cracking? Peeling?
12. Signs of insects. Sawdust? Mounds? Frass? Tunnels? Fresh exit holes?
13. Splash back. Dirt buildup on lower walls?

Window and Door Condition

1. Trim in good condition? Coated? Sealed to logs?
2. Exterior gaps? Does the unit close all the way? Are there any cracks?

3. Exterior coating condition.

4. Manufacturer? Quality? Age?

Roofline Condition

1. Overall appearance. Humps? Valleys?

2. Gutters and downspouts.

3. Fascia condition. Coating? Secured? Gaps?

4. Roof material condition. Cupping? Cracking? Debris?

5. Valley flashing.

6. Snow/ice shield.

7. Chimneys, vents, and so forth. Flashed? Sealed?

Porch or Deck Condition

1. Railing. Coated? Secured to post/wall? Signs of decay?

2. Post condition. Decay? Finish condition? Splash back?

3. Attachment to main structure.

4. Flooring. Type? Condition?

5. Vapor barrier underneath?

Inside Inspection

With your notes on the exterior, let's move inside.

General Condition

1. Did the door stick as you were opening it?

2. Did you immediately detect a stale, damp odor?

3. Are there any large open spaces?

4. Is the overall feeling dark and dingy or light and airy?

Interior Log Condition

1. Logs clean? Coated?

2. Walls plumb?

3. Insects. Boring holes? Sawdust?

4. Joint gaps. Butt joints? Beam joints? Between log courses?

5. Signs of weather infiltration. Water stains?

Frame Wall Condition

1. Connections to log wall. Out of plumb?
2. Connections to beams. Settling?
3. Trimwork. Connection to log wall change? Connection to beam change? Uneven gaps and spaces?
4. Buckling? Bowing?
5. Interior doors. Closing/latching? Clearance at the bottom?
6. Sheetrock. Cracking? Mildew?
7. Kitchen cabinets. Connection to wall change?
8. Countertop. Connection to wall change?

Window and Door Condition

1. Opening, shutting. Sticking? Gaps? Locks work?
2. Trimwork. Connection to logs? Bowing? Buckling?

Wet Wall Condition

1. Kitchen sink. Stale odor under cabinet? Water stains? Insects? Dishwasher? Refrigerator?
2. Clothes washer. Stale odor? Stains? Insects? Water connections? Laundry sinks?
3. Bathroom sink. Odor? Stains? Insects? Connections? Shower? Tub?

Floor Condition

1. Overlay? Seams?
2. Settling?
3. Upper level. Settling? Doors close and latch?

Post Condition

1. Connections. Buckling? Bowing? Movement?

Ceiling Condition

1. Purlins. Ridge beam. Bowing, twisting? Connection?
2. Log truss. Wall connection? Other connections?

Other Conditions

1. Fireplace, chimney. Floor connection? Shifting? Ceiling connection?
2. Large openings. Sagging above? Reveal on trimwork?
3. Bearing walls into the basement. Location? Sagging?
4. French/patio doors. Sticking? Close and latch? Reveal on trimwork?
5. Wall hangings, large furniture. What is behind them?
6. Wall to gable end connection. Condition? Bowing? Shifting?
7. Recent renovations. Why?

Basement/Crawl Space Condition

1. Stale odor? Ventilated?
2. Subfloor/ceiling. Sagging? Damp?
3. Recent renovations. Why?
4. Insulation.
5. Plumbing. Buckling? Mineral deposits?
6. Plastic on ground in crawl space (vapor barrier)?
7. Bearing walls/piers. Plumb? Condition?
8. Cracks in foundation walls? Water seepage? Insect signs?

This list is meant to serve as a preliminary survey of your home. The items on it pertain to log structure and maintenance. A home inspection professional should have a much more complete list for a thorough home inspection.

Inspection Discussion

Why was it important for us to go through all those items in the survey? Because log building techniques are not as commonplace as stick framing, and you have to understand *how* a log home works. Also, you can get lost in the beauty of a log home only to find out later you have problems and overpaid for the property. As you read through the different conditions and what to look for, keep this thought in mind: *A vast majority of problems with log homes are cosmetic and can be fixed.* A log home, as we have already discussed, must acclimate to its surroundings. This includes shrinking, settling, and adjusting. Logs are very strong and resilient. Once acclimated, all they need is care.

Outside Inspection

Site Condition

The type of soil is not a big issue, but it is an indicator of how well the site drains after a rainstorm or in the spring as the snow melts. You want to make sure the soil is graded *away* from your house. The steeper the better, but you do not want pockets (or puddles) of moisture resting against your foundation. That can lead to cracks in the foundation walls and water seepage, which in turn can lead to insect infestations and foundation failure. Vegetation against your log walls does not allow for adequate airflow, which is vital when the logs get wet. Your logs need to dry out after they get wet or they become an invitation to fungi and insects. Cut the vegetation back to the height of the foundation wall and 2 feet from the wall. I don't advocate getting rid of it altogether, because some vegetation lessens splash back on log walls from a rainstorm.

Insect infestations usually start somewhere outside the house. Look for signs and areas where insects lie in wait. You may spot tunnels of mud leading up the foundation wall or mounds in the soil. If you find these signs, consider treating the soil with a fumigant or insecticide injection. You will definitely find insects in woodpiles leaning against the house. Destroy the tunnels and mounds and move the woodpile at least 15 to 20 feet away from the house. Inspect the wall logs behind the woodpile for soft, punky wood. You can do this by tapping on the wood with a scratch awl or screwdriver. A resonating sound means there is solid wood. A dull, hollow thud means punky wood. During the inspection process, you are concerned only with identifying problems. The time will come to establish the extent of the problem. Read more about specific problems in Chapter 5.

Foundation/Subfloor Condition

There are many types of foundations and foundation materials. Some lend themselves more to settling problems than others. Proper construction techniques and materials are a good sign of what to expect throughout the rest of the inspection. This information helps to develop a whole picture. Because logs shrink and swell, it is important to look at the subfloor and how it is connected to the foundation. I have seen homes that have shifted to a dangerous position on the foundation. Check connections and the condition of the sill facing. Most codes call for a sill seal—a thin insulation strip between the sill plate and the foundation—look for this as a sign of paying attention to detail. The sill flashing should have been installed at the same time. Sill flashing is a thin strip of metal installed between the sill sealer and sill plate. It serves primarily as an insect shield. This is another sign that someone was paying attention.

Log Wall Condition

The first impression when looking at a log wall is its overall appearance. Does it look maintained? Does it look like it was laid up right? If there are butt joints, (where two logs come together in the same course) have they shifted? Do they match? Are they staggered in adjoining courses? Staggering butt joints in adjoining courses is an important structural issue, as this allows for a stronger interlocking structure and draws little away from passing most of the structural loads to the corners. Strength in a log home comes from the corners. Loads are transferred from the roof to the walls to the corners. From there loads transfer to the foundation. Log walls bow mainly from heavy loads caused by poor design or poor construction. Do the walls start at least 12 inches (preferably 18 inches) above ground level? This helps keep the logs dry and lessens splash back or a buildup of dirt on the lower courses. Now, look at the log texture. Is it rough? Smooth? Rough logs usually mean a drier, lower grade of milling on the logs. You guessed it, smooth means a greener, higher grade of milling. This is not an absolute rule, just a general rule of thumb. If the logs have been treated regularly to a coating of water repellent stain, you will notice it immediately. Gray, weathered logs will show a rougher texture, more aggressive large checks, and lots of small cracks. Dry, weathered logs are not considered to be a major problem. But, because most home owners want a clean, fresh look, this surface will have to be removed. The good news is, an untreated wall is easier to bring back to a newer look than a freshly stained wall. More importantly though, gray, weathered logs are an indication of lack of maintenance and a red flag that other problems may exist, like decay, rot, and insects.

Sometimes decay is not readily apparent, so you will have to "knock on wood" to find it. With the handle of your scratch awl, start tapping on wood surfaces. Pay particular attention to areas around the base of windows and doors, corner log extensions, other log ends, checks, and behind vegetation. Look also at areas of discoloration in the logs (particularly splash back areas), where there was a woodpile or anything else covering the logs. If there are signs of decay and rot, look also for signs of insect infestation, such as fresh boring holes and piles of sawdust and saw scat or frass on the logs. (Saw scat and frass are insect excretions that look like sawdust but are found on logs, usually around the boring hole.) Again, this is the process of identifying the problems. The scope of log damage is discussed in Chapter 6.

Look at the caulking and/or chinking. Does it pull away from the logs easily? Are there gaps where the material has pulled away from the logs on its own? This is an adhesion failure. Has the material developed stress tears in itself? This is a cohesion failure and probably the sign of an old, worn-out sealant bead. Look also for signs of obvious weather infiltration. These include open gaps, seeing daylight into the inside, and water stains.

Window and Door Condition

Windows and doors are usually associated with problems concerning air and water infiltration into the house. If the units have lost their efficiency, they may be inviting problems with the logs. If the units allow water into the house, they are most likely allowing water down behind the jambs. Cupping trim boards is a sign of a problem behind the trim. Mold and mildew on the unit itself is another sign.

If you know who the manufacturer is and the quality or grade selected by the home owner, you can determine the service life of those units.

Roofline Condition

Next to the logs, the roofline is the most prominent feature on a log home. The roofline can be the biggest indicator of shifting and settling in the log walls. Look for humps and valleys along the ridge or peak. Now stand below a sidewall and look *up* the rafter line to the peak. Look for any humps and valleys following the rafter line. Note where these are all occurring. There are many factors that could be contributing to these humps and valleys, many of which do not affect the home's structural integrity. However, if the walls are settling, the roofline condition could be a major repair issue. In the case of wall logs settling, look for settling jacks under posts and settling gaps over windows, doors, and on interior bearing walls. Valley flashing, snow and ice shields, gutters, and downspouts are more signs of quality construction, as they allow for proper water and snow runoff.

Another area for water seepage is around chimneys, vents, and other assemblies protruding from or attached at the roofline. Look for flashing and a sealed seam around the perimeter of these items.

Porch and Deck Condition

The major issues with porches and decks is their ability to pull away from the main structure. This is usually evidenced by a larger-than-normal gap between the house and the decking and also railing sections pulling away from support posts. Even though it might not be seen so readily, posts may be out of plumb, too. Look at the material used to construct the porch or deck. If the substructure is pressure-treated lumber, you won't be looking at replacing it any time soon. Look at the ground under the porch or deck. Is there a vapor barrier (a sheet of plastic 6 millimeters or thicker with a small amount of fill covering it)? The vapor barrier aids air circulation under the porch or deck by not allowing ground moisture to fuel a humid environment. A vapor barrier is recommended only when the porch or deck is within about 24 inches of ground level or there is considered to be inadequate ventilation. Is there any rotted debris under there? This is an excellent place for insects to stage their attack on the structure. While under there (or flashing a light into the space), look for signs of cracks in the foundation wall. This is another sign for moisture and insect infiltration.

Inside Inspection

General Condition

The first thing to ask yourself as you walk inside is does the door stick. This is usually a sign that the settling gap above the door is not wide enough to accommodate the wall log settling. As you walk through the entire house, keep your nose engaged. Do you smell a stale, damp odor? This is a good indicator of mold, mildew, or some kind of fungus. Now, look around. Are there any large open spaces, like a great room, or an area with a cathedral ceiling? Open spaces are not a problem; how they are supported is. A structural engineer could write a book on this subject alone, but here is a simple test. If you hear a squeaking, groaning sound coming from the top of the walls on a windy day or night, call in the professionals. The periodic popping sounds you hear do not qualify. They are the sounds of logs releasing their moisture as the house is acclimating.

Interior Log Condition

Taking an honest look at the interior log walls is sometimes a hard chore. Most people love log homes because they are relaxing and comfortable. Getting past that feeling is sometimes hard. But at some point, look at the interior log walls to confirm what you saw on the outside. Have the logs been coated with stain or some kind of finish? Have the joints been sealed with caulk or chink? Check for adhesion and cohesion failures here. Are there any obvious signs of weather infiltration, like water stains? In other words, have the logs been taken care of? Are the walls plumb? Do they bow at any point? Look also for signs of insect damage. Are there any fresh boring holes? Are there small piles of sawdust on the floor? Saw scat or frass on the logs? Are the butt joints and beam joints tight? Sealed?

Frame Wall Condition

If you have identified any potential problems with the interior log walls, you will most likely find problems with the frame walls. The first place to look is at the intersection of these walls with the log walls. Are they still tight (assuming they were constructed that way to begin with)? Has the trimwork pulled away or adjusted at all? It is not unusual to find this condition, and it is not a structural problem. Next look at the connection between the frame wall and any upper-level beam. Has or have the beam(s) sagged? Are there any cracks in the Sheetrock? Have any of the walls buckled or bowed? These are signs of settling. Look at the interior doors. Do they open and shut without sticking? Is the gap at the bottom of the doors uniform? Move to the kitchen. Look at the cabinet connection to the log walls. Does the same situation exist with the trim that you found with the frame walls?

Window and Door Condition

Do all of the windows and doors open and shut without sticking? Do the locks latch? Is the trimwork condition on the inside the same as on the outside? I once worked on a house in Colorado. On the day I arrived, as we were doing our initial walk-through, I noticed that the windows were ugly, dirty, the seal had broken on some of the thermopanes, and the windows were misted. I asked what they were going to do with the windows and the owner said nothing. I was thinking I should say something when his wife smiled and said the new windows were going to be delivered the next day. Sometimes a problem is not a problem.

Wet Wall Condition

Next to log sealing and finishing, wet wall condition is probably the area of biggest concern. Look at plumbing connections all over the house. You are looking for leaks. If you find a leak, try to figure out how long it has been leaking. Tap and probe the logs behind these connections. If they are solid and dry, you've just avoided an expensive repair.

Floor Condition

Floors are notorious for settling, buckling, and bowing in any structure. Depending on the severity of the problem, different remedies exist. If all your doors close and latch, this is not an issue. Extensive settling, on the other hand, is a structural issue best left to a professional.

Post Condition

One of the main reasons for humps and valleys in a roof system are the posts supporting them. Check the base of the posts for settling jacks that may need to be adjusted. Also, check the posts for plumb. A slightly out-of-plumb post that hasn't moved is not a structural issue. One that has moved and is not secured is. Checking for plumb is done by checking the base and top of the post for any movement. If the post is a manufactured cylinder, plumb is measured by placing a 4-inch or 6-inch-level against the post on at least two sides. If the post is a natural, tapered log, a quick test is to imagine a straight line from the base to the top in the middle of the post and place your level on it. If at all practical, drop a string line or plumb bob from the center of the top of the post.

Ceiling Condition

The main reason for humps and valleys goes to the ceiling. Because of log movement, log purlins and rafters will bow, twist, and warp. All they need to do is acclimate and settle. In most cases, this is not a structural issue and is not cost effective to remedy. Structural issues occur when connections start pulling apart. If this happens, you need a professional contractor.

Other Conditions

To ferret out other conditions, look for wall hangings, large furniture, and recent renovations. I have seen instances where these items were put in position to hide something. Look behind them.

Basement and Crawl Space Condition

Winding up the inspection tour, move to the basement or outside to look at the crawl space. In the basement do you notice a stale, damp odor? Is it clean? Well ventilated? Check the condition of the support posts or bearing walls. Are they plumb? Have they moved? Are there cracks in the walls? Mineral deposits on plumbing are usually an indication of a leak. Is the leak caused by the plumbing not adjusting to the house settling? If you are inspecting a crawl space, does the ground have a vapor barrier to protect against moisture and insects?

One of the nice features to log home living is that a handy home owner can remedy most of the situations we have discussed above. All you need is proper direction. Now that you have identified what is right and what is wrong with the structure, let's move on.

Chapter 3

Initial Applications

Initial Log Cleaning

Clean, sound, dry logs are the secret to a proper, long-lasting finish on log components. To achieve this, the logs first have to be cleaned. There are two basic methods used to clean logs:

> Wet—power washing and/or chemical stripping
>
> Dry—media blasting

Use the wet method if weathering is apparent, there is no existing finish coat, and to remove mold and mildew. Follow with an application of a preservative. Use the dry method if heavy weathering is apparent or if there is an existing finish coat. Follow with an application of a preservative. (See the section on "Stripping Methods" in Chapter 4 for a description of the process of media blasting.)

The main disadvantage of the wet method is the time needed to allow the logs to dry before applying stain. The dry method, while gaining in popularity, has one disadvantage. This method will remove visible signs of mold and mildew, but it may not kill the spores that propagate the condition. As a result, the affected areas may need to be treated with a bleach solution.

Regardless of the method chosen, the advantages of log cleaning include the following:

1. Clean, sound, dry logs accept a stain and sealant more readily.
2. Both methods produce a roughened texture on log surfaces. This is considered the best texture for today's log home exterior stains.
3. You have a clean surface to start with. You can confidently apply subsequent products, (preservatives, finishes, sealants) for better adhesion and penetration.
4. Cleaning not only works to remove dirt, mold, and mildew. Cleaning also removes mill glaze (from the manufacturing process) and oils from handling.

As you read through the chart on cleaners (see Figure 3–1), you will notice that the different types of cleaners generally have cleaning situations best suited for their formulations. The *sodium percarbonate bleaches* are gaining in popularity, while the *chlorine bleaches* are losing. Studies have shown that while chlorine bleaches clean and sterilize log surfaces, they also damage wood fibers. Percarbonates do the same job but without the damage. You may already be familiar with this concept. Have you seen the "oxygen" bleach commercials on television? Oxygen bleaches fall into the category of sodium percarbonate bleaches.

The wet method of cleaning logs involves the following steps:

1. Working one wall at a time, wet the logs with a garden hose or sprayer. You do not have to saturate the logs, just get the surfaces wet. This will minimize any streaking that could occur and opens the fibers to better accept the cleaner. As with any new project, start at the back of the house.

2. Mix the cleaner as instructed by the manufacturer.

3. Starting at the bottom of the wall, apply the mixture, using a pump-up garden sprayer, to a section of the wall that can be worked in a ten to fifteen minute time frame. Some manufacturers suggest leaving the cleaner on the logs for a short period before brushing. The reason for starting at the bottom is that liquefied cleaners will streak on dry log material and thus can be harder to remove.

4. Using a soft bristled brush, work the mixture in, paying particular attention to the dirty and stained sections.

5. *Thoroughly* rinse off the section using a power washer.

6. Once the entire wall is done, rinse the wall again.

Repeat these steps until the entire structure is cleaned.

You will probably find that regardless of the cleaner chosen, the more aggressive you are with the cleaner—brushing it in and rinsing it off—the more you will find a fuzzy, roughened texture to the logs when you are done. Although a roughened texture is advantageous for subsequent applications, too rough a texture could mean one of two things:

1. Your cleaner has been left on the logs too long. Shorten the time frame of working the mixture in before rinsing.

2. The PSI setting on your pressure washer is too high. If you cannot reduce the setting to 1,500 PSI or lower, try using a garden hose.

Unless the next step is the application of a preservative, allow the logs to dry completely. This could take several days. The logs should be dry to the touch, with no wet spots. Wet spots are usually found around checks, cracks, and in the corners. Don't be discouraged; an advantage of this method is that by identifying these wet spots, potential problem areas are also identified. These areas will require extra attention when the time comes to apply the finish and sealants.

Chlorine Bleach

Sodium hypochlorite or household bleach generally mixed no stronger than 1:3 with water. *Calcium hypochlorite* is a more concentrated bleach used in pools or spas generally mixed 2-3 oz. to 1 gal. of water. Do not let these mixes stay on log surfaces more than 10–15 minutes before rinsing them off. *Sodium hydroxide* cleaners are classified in this category.

Pros	Cons
Cheap	Chlorine gas can be released if mixed with other household
Readily available	chemicals such as ammonia.
Kills mildew	Chlorine gas can be hazardous or fatal
Bleaches all types of wood	Readily kills plants, especially new growth
	Can over-oxidize wood cell walls and degrade them
	Very corrosive to metal fasteners, such as nails and screws.
	If not completely rinsed from the surface of the wood, it can degrade the top layer of wood fibers, causing failure in the applied coating.

Oxalic Acid

A naturally occurring acid found in many plans. Very good at removing iron, nail and tannin stains. Best used on bare wood. Existing coatings should be completely removed in order for this cleaner to have proper affect. Comes in crystal form and generally mixed at 2 cups per gallon of water. Hot water dissolves the crystals faster.

Pros	Cons
Particularly good at removing tannin stains	Does not kill mildew
It is the product of choice on redwood only	It is a poison and must be handled very carefully
It is the best product for removing rust stains	It must be thoroughly rinsed from the wood that will be finished with water based coatings. Otherwise, whitish blemishes appear

Sodium Percarbonate Bleach

Based on *hydrogen peroxide,* percarbonates are usually sold in powder/liquid form. Mixed with water, it becomes an aggressive cleaner.
Applied to log surfaces, let the mix stand for 15 minutes before working with a soft brush. Also known as *Oxygen Bleach.*

Pros	Cons
Environmentally friendly	Will turn unaged redwood almost black in color
Safest to use (may irritate the eyes)	More expensive than other cleaners/bleaches
Does not aggressively corrode metal fasteners	If not rinsed completely, residual soda ash can appear as
Disassociates into hydrogen peroxide, soda ash and	whitish patches under stain
water	
Kills mildew	
Strongly bleaches all types of wood—except unaged redwood	

Trisodium Phosphate

Or TSP, a product for cleaning dirt, grease or wax. May darken some woods but can be brightened using an oxygen bleach solution. Recommended as a cleaner for removing wax; used in most paints/stains for water repellency. Generally mixed at 1/2 cup per gallon of water.

Pros	Cons
Readily available	No bleaching action
Inexpensive	
Good for cleaning dirt	

Potassium Salts of Fatty Acids

Also called *soap salts.* Marketed as a moss and algae concentrate, or an insecticidal soap. This is a specific use product, used only when the problem is identified as a moss, algae, lichen.

Pros	Cons
Readily available	Not considered for general use on the entire structure.
Inexpensive	No bleaching action
Low toxicity but will cause eye irritation	
Toxic to certain insects in their immature stage only.	

Courtesy of Sashco Sealants—1/8/01

Figure 3–1. Log Cleaner Comparison Chart.

If, however, you are going to apply a borate preservative, the logs do not have to be dry. In fact, this type of preservative is best applied while the logs are still wet.

When done, make sure to clean the equipment thoroughly. Tools used to apply waterborne cleaners clean easily in warm, soapy water.

The section on "Stripping Methods" in Chapter 4 describes the method of media blasting. However, it is worth noting here that media blasting is usually best left to a professional. Most rental store compressors and media blasters do not generate the necessary power to perform this job adequately.

Cleaners *v* Brighteners

Research has come so far that some product categories now have subcategories. Such is the case with log cleaners and log brighteners.

Log Cleaners

Log cleaners are usually formulated with a higher concentration of a bleaching agent, detergent, and oxidizing agent. The bleaching agents used are either a chlorine bleach (sodium or calcium hypochlorite) or an oxygen bleach (sodium percarbonate). Chlorine bleaches have been shown to damage wood fibers, so oxygen bleaches are the more popular bleach used. In addition, *hydrogen peroxide* or *sodium hydroxide* is added to act as an oxidizing agent. An oxidizing agent is a chemical that counteracts the weathering process and restores the original color of the wood. In some cases though, the sodium hydroxide will darken the wood. Because of the concentration of bleach, a log cleaner is the best choice when removing mildew stains is important.

Log Brighteners

Log brighteners are formulated more for their oxidizing powers than their cleaning powers. Log brighteners usually contain *oxalic acid,* which is used mainly to counteract sodium hydroxide and the effects of extractive bleeding and iron stain. Brighteners are also used to neutralize log surfaces after caustic chemical strippers have been used. You can read more about these conditions in Chapter 5 in the section on "Finish Failure."

Preserving Logs

Log preservation techniques are meant to protect logs against decay organisms caused by fungi and insect infestations. That does not include molds and mildews. There are some borate class preservatives that contain moldicides. Because we are dealing with both molds and mildews, they are dealt with in the section on "Choosing an Exterior Wood Finish." Mildewcides are normally additives to stain finishes.

As Figure 3–2 demonstrates, the majority of home owner applied preservatives are in the borate class. They are inexpensive, easy to apply, easy to clean up after, and are for unrestricted use. This means the home owner can apply the preservative without regulatory issues concerning professional application only.

Because borate preservatives penetrate wet wood more thoroughly, you don't have to wait once you are done cleaning the logs. If you have elected not to clean the logs or you used a dried media blaster, wet the walls down prior to applying the preservative. A garden hose works best.

Borate preservatives should not be applied in direct sunlight or when it is raining. Application temperature ranges are generally 40° to 90°F. This range is for substrate surface or log material temperature, not air temperature. Depending on the building location, especially in sunny environments, it is not uncommon to have an air temperature that is 10° to 15°F *lower* when the log surface temperature is at 40°F. In other words, the ideal time to apply the preservative is on a cool, cloudy, relatively humid day. However, ideal situations are rare, so keep track of the sun movement, start on a shaded wall, and work around the house as the sun passes. If the preservative mixture

Name	Registered	Active Ingredient	Application	Note
Timbor	U.S. Borax	disodium octaborate tetrahydrate	1 lb. to 1 gal. water	spray or brush application
Penetreat	Sashco Products	disodium octaborate tetrahydrate	1 lb. to 1 gal. water	10% solution
Bora-Care	Nisus Corp.	disodium octaborate tetrahydrate ethylene glycol	from container	spray or brush application 20% solution
Jecta	Nisus Corp.	disodium octaborate tetrahydrate ethylene glycol	from container	40% solution injectable
Bora-col 20-2	Sansin Corp.	disodium octaborate tetrahydrate monopropylene glycol	from container	20% solution spray or brush application
Bora-col 20-2 BD	Sansin Corp.	disodium octaborate tetrahydrate monopropylene glycol didecyl dimethyl ammonium chloride	from container	20% solution spray or brush application moldicide
Bora-col 10-2 BD	Sansin Corp.	disodium octaborate tetrahydrate monopropylene glycol didecyl dimethyl ammonium chloride	from container	moldicide
Impel Rod	Chemical Specialties Corp.	anhydrous disodium octaborate polybor	insert in pre-drilled holes	fused rod
Shell-Guard	Perma-Chink Systems, Inc.	propylene glycol polyethylene glycol disodium octaborate tetrahydrate	from container	spray or brush application 20% solution
Armor-Guard	Perma-Chink Systems, Inc.	disodium octaborate tetrahydrate	1 lb. to 1 gal. water	10% solution

Figure 3–2. Different formulations of borate preservatives.

Toxicity of Common Materials & Pesticides

Material	Acute Oral LD50 (mg/kg)*	
Nicotine	10	
Diazinon	100	
Gasoline	150	
Caffeine	200	
Sevin	650	**More**
Aspirin	1200	**Toxic**
Malathion	1375	
Impel Rod	1760	**Less**
Timbor	2500	**Toxic**
Table salt	3320	
Boric acid	3500	
BoraCare concentrate	5000+	
Jecta	5000+	
Niban (calculated)	60,000+	

The lower the number, the more toxic the material

This chart courtesy of Preservation Research Group, Inc.-updated 7/25/02

Figure 3–3. Borate toxicity.

evaporates too quickly leaving a dusty, crystallized film on the log components, lightly mist the components to maintain a wet surface.

Borate preservatives, especially those supplied in powder form, are generally applied twice. The second application goes on before the first one has dried. You can tell if the water is evaporating too fast by signs of a powdery film forming on the logs. You can either mist the logs a few times until the sun moves, or you can sweep the film off with a broom or brush.

The actual applications themselves are best done with a garden sprayer or an airless sprayer. Do not use a pressure washer here because pressure is not the key, volume is. The proper application is to apply to "the point of refusal." In other words, spray the log components slowly until the logs will not soak up any more and the mixture starts to run off the components. This is also referred to as *flooding*.

As the preservative is being applied, pay particular attention to checks, butt joints, log ends, and log members close to the ground. Saturating these components provides more protection, especially in the checks.

If there are log or other wood members 6 inches or less from the ground, consider using a higher concentration of the preservative mixture, Impel Rods or Jecta, or a combination of these. The log and other

Sample	Registered	Active Ingredient	Effective	Notes
Polyphase	Troy Corp.	3-iodo-2-propynyl butyl carbamate	molds, mildews, fungal decay	~.5% by weight, several commercial
	Olin Corp.			WRPs, both solvent and water based
Cuprinol #20	Cuprinol, NA	zinc naphthenate	mildews, fungal decay	~2% by weight, several WRP's, solvent and water based
Cuprinol #10	Cuprinol, NA	copper naphthenate	ground contact, fungal decay	~2% by weight, several WRP's, imparts green coloring
Woodguard	ISK, Bioscience	copper-8-quinolinolate	molds, mildews, fungal decay	.25%-.675% by weight, imparts green/brown color
TBTO	Walla Walla	bis tributyltin oxide	molds, mildews, fungal decay	.5%–1% by weight, several WRP's

Figure 3–4. Other commercially available preservatives.

wood members referred to include bottoms of posts, stair stringers, the bottom stair tread, the bottom of railings, and the lowest two to three courses of wall logs. Even if the bottom corner log ends are higher than 6 inches from ground level, it is a good idea to treat these with an extra dose of preservatives. Directions come with the products, so read them carefully.

Is this overkill? Probably, but it is better to be safe than sorry.

Most important, before applying the stain finish, the logs must be clean, dry, and sound. Waiting for the log components to dry may take several days, but the entire structure must be dry. Most stain finishes have some form of water repellent, such as a paraffinic wax or oil. If the finish is applied over damp logs, the wax will trap moisture under the finish and cause finish failure. Either the finish will not develop good adhesion to the log substrate and/or the trapped moisture will crack and cause peeling of the finish as it tries to escape. Don't take the chance that trapped moisture will be handled by the borates. Because this situation is easy to spot, a failed finish application is not going to be covered by any warranty.

Choosing an Exterior Wood Finish

The following excerpt is an excellent discussion on choosing an exterior wood finish. It can be found in its entirety in *The Wood Handbook: Wood as an Engineering Material*, Gen. Tech. Rep. FPL-GTR-113, Madison, Wisconsin: U.S. Department of Agriculture, Forest Service, Forest Products Laboratory, 1999.

The entire chapter takes up thirty-six pages, and it includes topics not applicable to this book. I have excerpted only those passages I felt give a general description of the product groups to choose from.

45

Following the excerpt is a chart from the same book showing the main features of each type. Not included in the chart, but offered as a further breakdown of finish types are the terms *waterborne, oil-borne, water-based,* and *oil-based. Solvent* is sometimes used interchangeably with *oil,* i.e. solvent-borne, solvent-based. The term *borne* refers to the carrying agent for application and cleanup, while *based* refers to the effective formulation for penetration or surface coating. Until recently water and oil could not be mixed, so *borne* and *based* held the same meaning. Because water cleanup is much more popular and friendly, recent technology has allowed the mixing of waterborne with oil-based. More simply put, waterborne = water cleanup, oil-borne = solvent cleanup, water-based = surface coating stain, oil-based = penetrating stain.

> The types of exterior finishes for wood are separated into two groups, those that penetrate wood and those that form a film. A general rule, penetrating finishes tend to give a more "natural" look to the wood. They have a smaller concentration of "solids" that protect log surfaces from UV radiation. That is, they allow some of the character of the wood, i.e. grain, to show through the finish. Semitransparent, penetrating stains have a slightly larger concentration of solids. Also, the more natural a finish, the less durable it is. Natural finishes may be penetrating finishes such as varnish, linseed oil and tung oil. The penetrating natural finishes generally give better performance and are easier to refinish. . . .
>
> . . . Penetrating finishes constitute a broad classification of natural wood finishes that do not form a film on the wood surface. Penetrating finishes are classified as (a) transparent or clear systems, (b) lightly colored systems, (c) pigmented or semitransparent systems, and (d) oils.
>
> (a) . . . Transparent or clear finishes are generally a type of water repellent or water repellent preservative. Preservatives differ from repellents in that they contain a fungicide . . .
>
> . . . Water repellent preservatives maintain the original appearance of the wood, but they are not very durable . . . The first application of a water repellent preservative may protect exposed wood surfaces for only 1 to 2 years, but subsequent reapplications may last 2 to 4 years because the weathered boards absorb more finish.
>
> (b) . . . Lightly colored finishes may be water or solvent-borne formulations. The color may be obtained from dyes or finely ground pigments. Although they are still classified as a penetrating finish or sealer for wood, many of the newer formulations form a slight film on the wood surface . . . Although their durability is improved by the inclusion of UV stabilizers and finely ground pigment, lightly colored finishes still lack sufficient pigment to stop UV degradation of the wood.

(c) . . . Inorganic pigments can also be added to water repellent preservative solutions to provide special color effects, and the mixture is then classified as a semitransparent stain . . . The addition of pigments to the finish helps stabilize the color and increase the durability of the finish, but they give a less natural appearance because the pigment partially hides the original grain and color of the wood. Semitransparent stains are generally much more durable than are water repellent preservatives and provide more protection against weathering . . . The amount of pigment in semitransparent stains can vary considerably, thus providing different degrees of protection against UV degradation and masking of the original wood surface. Higher pigment concentration yields greater protection against weathering, but it also hides the natural color of the wood.

Solvent-borne oil-based semitransparent penetrating stains penetrate the wood surface, are porous, and do not form a surface film like paints. As a result, they will not blister or peel even if moisture moves through the wood. Semitransparent penetrating stains are only moderately pigmented and do not totally hide the wood grain. Penetrating stains are alkyd or oil based, and some may contain a fungicide as well as a water repellent.

Moderately pigmented latex-based (waterborne) stains are also available, but they do not penetrate the wood surface as well as the oil-based stains. Some latex-based formulations are oil modified. These formulations give better penetration than do the unmodified formulations . . . Efforts are continuing to improve these formulations; it is advisable to check with a local paint supplier for the latest developments in this area.

(d) . . . Drying oils, such as linseed and tung, are sometimes used by themselves as natural finishes. Such oils are not recommended for exterior use unless they are formulated with a mildewcide. These oils are natural products and therefore provide food for mildew.

Clear varnish is the primary transparent film-forming material used for a natural wood finish, and it greatly enhances the natural beauty and figure of wood. However, varnish lacks exterior permanence unless protected from direct exposure to sunlight, and varnish finishes on wood exposed outdoors without protection will generally require refinishing every 1 to 2 years.

Several finish manufacturers have formulated varnish with finely ground inorganic pigments that partially block UV radiation yet allow much of the visible light to pass through the finish . . . The degradation of the pigmented varnish initially occurs on the film surface as crazing and checking . . . Eventually, however, the buildup of coats will block much of the visible light and the wood will appear black.

Solid-color stains are opaque finishes (also called hiding, heavy-bodied, or blocking) that come in a wide range of colors and are

Initial application and maintenance of exterior wood finishes[1]

| Finish | Initial Application | | Appearance of wood | Maintenance | | |
	Process	Cost		Process	Cost	Service life[2]
Water repellent preservative	Brushing	Low	Grain visible; wood brown to black, fades slightly with age	Brush to remove surface dirt; remove mildew	Low	1–3 years
Waterborne preservative[3]	Pressure (factory applied)	Medium	Grain visible; wood greenish or brownish, fades with age	Brush to remove surface dirt; remove mildew	Nil, unless stained or painted	None, unless stained, or painted
Organic solvent preservative[4]	Pressure, steeping, dipping, and brushing	Low to medium	Grain visible; color as desired	Brush and reapply	Medium	2–3 years or when preferred
Water repellent[5]	One or two brush coats of clear material or, preferably, dip application	Low	Grain and natural color visible, becoming darker and rougher textured with age	Clean and reapply	Low to Medium	1–3 years or when preferred
Semitransparent stain	One or two brush coats	Low to medium	Grain visible; color as desired	Clean and reapply	Low to medium	3–6 years or when preferred
Clear varnish	Three coats (minimum)	High	Grain and natural color unchanged if adequately maintained	Clean, sand, and stain bleached areas; apply two more coats	High	2 years or at breakdown
Solid color stain	Brushing; water repellent, two top coats	Medium to high	Grain and natural color obscured	Clean and apply top coat, or remove and repeat initial treatment if damaged	Medium	3–7 years

[1]Compilation of data from observation of many researchers.

[2]For vertical exposure

[3]Although wood treated with waterborne preservative may be left unfinished, it is best to finish it with water-repellent preservative or semitransparent stain.

[4]Pentachlorophenal, bis(tri-n-butyltin oxide), copper naphthenate, copper-8-quinolinolate, or similar materials.

[5]With or without added preservatives. Addition of preservative helps control mildew growth.

Reprinted: *The Wood Handbook: Wood as an Engineering Material,* U.S. Dept. of Agriculture, Forest Service, Forest Products Laboratory, FPL-GTR-113

Figure 3–5. Initial application and maintenance of exterior wood finishes

made with a much higher concentration of pigment than are semi-transparent penetrating stains. As a result, solid-color stains totally obscure the natural color and grain of the wood. Solid-color stains (both oil- and latex-based) tend to form a film much like paint, and as a result they can also peel from the substrate.

Author's note: Some log home stain manufacturers today are adopting a modified solid-color stain approach. The solid-color stain is formulated to expose some of the natural look and grain of the log surface. A second, or clear coat, is then applied to provide a water repellent shell that will also shrink and swell with the seasonal movement of the log components. Subsequent applications are then only concerned with reapplying the top coat over the existing finish and sealant. If the objective is to maintain a contrasting color scheme between the finish and sealant, this system seems to work extremely well.

Moisture-excluding effectiveness of various finishes on ponderosa pine*

Finish	No. of coats	Moisture-excluding effectiveness (%)			Finish	No. of coats	Moisture-excluding effectiveness (%)		
		1 day	7 days	14 days			1 day	7 days	14 days
Linseed oil sealer (50%)	1	7	0	0	Enamel, paint, stain	1	93	69	50
	2	15	1	0	(soya, tung, alkyd:	2	96	83	70
	3	18	2	0	interior/exterior)	3	97	86	80
Linseed oil	1	12	0	0		4	98	92	85
	2	22	0	0		5	98	93	88
	3	33	2	0		6	98	94	89
Tung oil	1	34	0	0	Floor and deck enamel	1	80	31	18
	2	46	2	0	(phenolic alkyd)	2	89	53	35
	3	52	6	2		3	92	63	46
Paste furniture wax	1	6	0	0	Shellac	1	65	10	3
	2	11	0	0		2	84	43	20
	3	17	0	0		3	91	64	42
Water repellent	1	12	0	0		4	93	75	58
	2	46	2	0		5	94	81	67
	3	78	27	11		6	95	85	73
Latex flat wall paint	1	5	0	0	Nitrocellulose lacquer	1	40	4	1
(vinyl acrylic resin)	2	11	0	0		2	70	22	8
	3	22	0	0		3	79	37	19
Latex primer wall paint	1	78	37	20	Floor seal	1	31	1	0
(butadiene-styrene resin)	2	86	47	27	(phenolic resin/tung oil)	2	80	37	18
	3	88	55	33		3	88	56	35
Alkyd latex house	1	43	6	1	Spar varnish	1	48	6	0
primer paint	2	66	14	2	(soya alkyd)	2	80	36	15
	3	72	20	4		3	87	53	30
Acrylic latex flat	1	52	12	5	Urethane varnish	1	55	10	2
house paint	2	77	28	11	(oil modified)	2	83	43	23
	3	84	39	16		3	90	64	44
Solid-color latex stain	1	5	0	0		4	91	68	51
(acrylic resin)	2	38	4	0		5	93	72	57
	3	50	6	0		6	93	76	62
Solid-color oil-based stain	1	45	7	1	Aluminum flake pigmented	1	90	61	41
(linseed oil)	2	84	48	26	urethane varnish	2	97	87	77
	3	90	64	42	(oil modified)	3	98	91	84
FPL natural finish (linseed-	1	62	14	3		4	98	93	87
oil-based semitransparent	2	70	21	6		5	98	94	89
stain)	3	76	30	11		6	99	95	90
Semitransparent oil-based	1	7	0	0	Polyurethane finish, clear	1	48	6	0
stain (commercial)	2	13	0	0	(two components)	2	90	66	46
	3	21	1	0		3	94	81	66
Marine enamel, gloss (soya	1	79	38	18	Polyurethane paint, gloss	1	91	66	44
alkyd)	2	91	66	46	(two components)	2	94	79	62
	3	93	74	57		3	96	86	74
Alkyd house primer paint	1	85	46	24	Paraffin wax, brushed	1	97	82	69
(tall maleic alkyd resin)	2	93	70	49	Paraffin wax, dipped	1	100	97	95
	3	95	78	60					

*Sapwood was initially finished and conditioned to 26°C (80°F) and 30% RH, then exposed to the same temperature and 90% RH.

Source: *The Wood Handbook: Wood as an Engineering Material.* Gen. Tech. Rep. FPL-GTR-113, Madison, WI: U.S. Department of Agriculture, Forest Service, Forest Products Laboratory, 1999.

Figure 3–6. Moisture-excluding effectiveness chart

Finish Application Tips

Because there are so many "systems" available on the market, this section offers some application techniques.

Before starting, a word of caution. It is very important to make sure that the caulk or chink used to seal log joints is compatible with the finish. If you are unsure, apply the caulk or chink *before* applying the

finish. Compatibility is an issue when it comes to adhesion of the sealing material to the wood. (See "Compatibility Issues" in Chapter 4.)

I have yet to find a finish, stain, or "system" that can't be applied
with either brushes, rollers, airless sprayers, or a combination of these.
So, first you have to decide what you want the finished applied product
to look like. No one ever wants to "just slop it on." Everyone wants a
quality job done. Unfortunately, quality means different things to different people. Even if for you definition of quality is on the lower end of the
scale, buy the best tools you can afford. Good brushes and rollers will
more than pay for themselves when you start using them. The big payoff
comes when the first compliment is made. That compliment will make
you forget how much you paid and how much time you spent working.

Tools

You will need the following tools: two to three different-size natural
bristle brushes, a Rubbermaid-type soft bristle utility brush with
broom handle, a roller with a medium and a smooth pad, a roller pan,
one to two one-gallon plastic pails, clean white cotton rags, several
rolls of $1^1/_2$- or 2-inch masking tape, cleaning materials for brushes

and rollers, a Masonite shield (described later), and don't forget the radio. An airless sprayer is an excellent tool for applying finish to wall logs. If you have access to one, it will dramatically shorten the time needed to complete this job. Don't forget to add eye protection and a respirator (the inexpensive fabric type will do) to the tool list.

Practice first on scrap material or hidden log components. Try spraying, brushing, and rolling to achieve the desired finish. Remember, the choice of color was based on a color chip or a brochure. The actual application to logs and trimwork *will* look different. It is important to practice and verify the finish look you want to achieve. A roller will generally leave the lightest coat, brushes are a little heavier, and sprayers will leave the heaviest coat.

Weather Considerations

Most importantly, make sure the temperature of the log surfaces are within the manufacturer's recommended application range. Usually the range is between 40°F and 90°F. Do not confuse air temperature with log surface temperature; it is not uncommon to find the surface temperature to be 50°F *higher* than the existing air temperature. Granted, this condition is found almost exclusively on log surfaces with direct exposure to sunlight, so work in the shade and allow the exposed log surfaces to cool down once the sunlight passes. I am aware of two methods to test log surfaces. One method is an adhesive-backed temperature strip available at paint stores. These are inexpensive and a good home owner item. The one I am familiar with is called temPAINTure. Following the directions, simply apply it to the surface to be finished and wait for a reading. The second method is a temperature gun with a laser-directed beam. This tool can be found in an auto parts store. These are a lot more expensive than the strips, but they give a more accurate reading, last longer, and have more uses. Whichever method you choose, it is a good idea to shoot several readings around the structure. This will help you determine when and where to apply the finish so that you get the best adhesion and curing rate. Then it is time to start applying the finish.

Back Brushing

The objective here is to apply an even coat over the entire surface. If you use an airless sprayer, you'll need two or three people to do the job. One person to apply the coating, and the others to "back brush" it. Back brushing is important because if done properly, it works the coating into the checks and cracks and evens out overspray, splatters, and lap joints. Even though it is virtually impossible to remove all lap

joints, an evenly textured coating presents much better than just applying it and not working it in. While working the finish in, brush left and right, up and down, dabbing into the tough spots. Always finish with a few soft strokes following the grain. Don't be timid about brushing. Be aggressive and work the finish in to all nooks, crannies, cracks, and crevices.

Applying the Finish

Now you want to think about the color scheme for the entire structure. Will everything be finished the same color or will there be accents such as roof trim and window and door trim? In an ideal situation, all trimwork has the finish applied *before* it is installed. This is fine for new construction, but what about existing homes? Sometimes, or should I say, most of the time, the color scheme is changed to suit the new home owners or a change in taste. In this case, the accent color is applied *after* the main color has been applied. For the sake of simplicity, the following application method describes a single color scheme, but it can be adapted for either color scheme.

Fascia

Starting at the top, apply the finish to the entire fascia first. It is best to do this before the finished roofing material is applied. Most fascia material is rough sawn, so use a 3 inch- or 4-inch natural bristle brush. If the finish "system" calls for multiple coats, apply these also. This will get you out of the roofer's way and give you a first look at how the house will finish out.

Soffit

Soffit material is usually a smoother-textured material, so the roller works best here. If you haven't run into this before, you will find that smoother surfaces accept stains differently than rougher surfaces. Smoother surfaces show brush marks or streaks more if the stain is applied the same way as on a rougher-textured surface. Starting at the back of the house, saturate the roller with stain, then roll out the excess in the pan to the point where you think you rolled out almost all of the stain. Roll some stain over a small area of the soffit. Make sure to use the same application you used on the practice pieces. Stain the entire soffit before moving on to the logs. Be careful not to roll stain onto the wall logs. The stain will dry and show up as a dark spot after the wall logs are coated. This can be mitigated by using a quarter-inch sheet of Masonite (see illustration) measuring about 12 by 20 inches as a shield. (Note: In the middle of one of the 12-inch sides, scribe and cut a radius matching your post diameter. It is not necessary to trace the entire diameter, just a concave surface to place against posts while

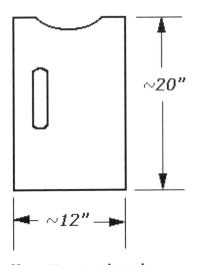

Masonite sprayboard

they are being stained.) As you move along, place the shield against the surface you don't want to stain. You will probably find the Masonite shield will help throughout the coating process. When done, save it for future applications.

As you are rolling the soffit, you will notice lap joints where you finished one run and started another. Lap joints are formed when you overlap a wet run over a previous run. Because you are most likely standing on a ladder or scaffolding, try these methods to avoid lap joints:

1. If the soffit material has staggered joints, stop the run at one of these joints, or as close as you can get.
2. If the soffit material is pine boards, roll one board at a time.
3. Roll as much as possible, the width of the roller, against the wall. Then, roll as much as possible a roller width away from the wall. Work your way out to the fascia. As you work your way out toward the fascia, stagger the point where you stop rolling with each line.
4. If the soffit material is solid and flat, change directions as you would when rolling out an interior wall.
5. Using a dry brush, brush out the lap joints in the same manner as described in the step above.
6. At the end of rolling a length, release pressure on the roller so that there is a lighter coating at the end of the roll. Overlap the next run, starting with light pressure.

If there are any exposed log members, such as purlins, ridge logs, collar ties, or log trusses, this might be a good time to stain these members. The decision should be based on the following points:

1. How many are there?
2. Can they be reached at the same time the soffit is being coated?
3. Are the wall logs going to brushed or sprayed? Application to these log members will need to be done the same way. The answer will determine the equipment you will need on the work platform.

As you coat these members, visually inspect and make a mental note on: (a) gaps in fascia and soffit materials, (b) log to soffit seams, (c) log ends under and behind the fascia, and (d) checks, dimples, and catfaces. These are the places that will need extra help to seal them against weather, insects, and birds. If and when future problems are experienced, these will be the first places to look. When the ladders, scaffolding, and genie lifts are gone, they will be harder and more expensive to fix. You can seal exposed log ends (i.e., log purlins) now or when the corner log ends are sealed. (See the section on "Applying the Sealant.")

Wall Logs

Moving on to the wall logs, start at the highest log and work down. It is best to coat the entire length of a log before moving down. When you get to the point where you cannot reach the entire length in one shot, here are the choices.

1. Using the methods to soften the lap joints, coat two, three, or four courses at the same time. Make sure to coat the entire length of these courses before moving down.
2. Set up additional scaffolding or plank-ways so that the entire length or a natural breaking point can be reached.

Between windows and doors, coat the entire section at the same time. Once low enough to where the logs are passing under a window, the window section is done. Staining from ground level is a lot easier, so as before, stain the entire length of the log or logs to the doorway or opposite corner.

I have found an airless sprayer is the best tool for coating wall logs. The process will go much faster and the material will be applied more evenly. If you choose this option, as my friend Wayne will tell you, "Don't forget to brush, because brushing is very important." Using a paintbrush is fine, but a soft-bristle utility brush by Rubbermaid attached to a broom handle works better. Finishing up the wall logs, don't forget to coat the bottom of the corner logs. Once at the corner logs, it is important to seal the log ends extending out past the corners. These log ends will absorb moisture faster than any other part of the log. If the coating system does not seal these ends, there are two choices. One is a commercial end sealer, the other is a slurry mix of caulking. (See "Exposed Log Ends" in chapter 6.)

Stain all the surfaces of each component before moving on to the next component. This will soften any variances experienced between the different components. First the fascia, then the soffit, then the wall logs, and so forth.

If this initial application is being completed at the time of construction, this is a good time to coat items like sill siding, trim boards, stair stringers, treads, and railing material. Again, an airless sprayer works best, but don't forget to brush. *Brushing is very important.* Once installed, these items are a lot harder to coat and the overspray or spatters can get on items you don't want the stain on. Touching up after these items are installed is a whole lot easier than staining them in place.

As the initial application is winding down, keep an eye out for places where future finish carpentry items will come in contact with already completed rough carpentry. These areas should be coated *before* the finish work is done. When the entire house project is complete, clean lines in these areas will give a more finished look to the house. These areas include:

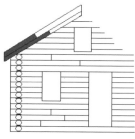

Step 1: Start high, use material breaks

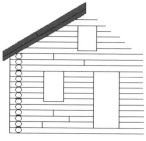

Step 2: Complete entire component

Step 3: Start high, work one section at a time

Step 4: Work down, one section at a time

Step 5: Work entire height before moving down

Step 6: Use breaks in material when working long sections

Step 7: Finish entire length before moving down

Step 8: Finish a complete section before taking a break

Step 9: Use breaks in material whenever possible

Step 10: Always work one section at a time

Step 11: Corner logs can be finished last

Step 12: Job done, clean your tools, take a break

1. where decking meets the house and around posts
2. where posts are seated against walls and on piers
3. around windows and doors, before the trimwork is applied
4. around electric, telephone, cable, and satellite connections and water spigots

Staining or coating support posts and touch-ups should be all that is left. If the material you use comes in five gallon pails, save one pail for future use and touch-ups.

Choosing a Sealant

Before we go any further, here is my philosophy concerning sealing log homes: *All log homes, regardless of age or production method used, will need to be sealed.*

Disagree if you would like. The bottom line is that log materials will continually shrink and swell over the life of the structure. Gaps will open up and weather will get in. Protect your investment and seal it—outside and inside.

The choice of an appropriate sealant is covered in the following products chart (see Figure 3.7). The objective of the chart is to point out the differences of the types available. The advantages of a proper sealant should be apparent, and your choice should be one of quality, not price.

Here the discussion is on application techniques. There are as many application techniques as there are sealants on the market. Most techniques differ by the material being used and individualized "tooling" techniques. As you become familiar with applying sealants, you will develop your own tooling techniques. The following techniques apply to synthetic materials in the *siliconized acrylic latex* class. You may also hear sealants referred to as *elastomeric*. This is a more generalized classification of sealants referring to a specialized formulation with a higher degree of flexibility. These are the most common materials used in log home sealing.

As with finish applications, the important decision is compatibility. Make sure the sealant you choose is compatible with the finish.

There are two types of synthetic sealant materials made specifically for log components: caulks and chinks.

The main decision for which sealant to use is the finished appearance. Caulks are a smoother or finer-textured material. When used to seal the seam between log courses, the finished appearance is generally up to half an inch wide and meant to be unnoticed or inconspicuous. I have used caulks in checks measuring 2 inches wide, and the appearance is smooth and glossy when a finish is applied. Chinks are a gritty, textured material generally used in beads up to 4 inches wide. While chinks are generally used to seal wider seams than caulks, the decision to use chink sealants may also include a desire for an offsetting appearance to the finish color used. Because of the size of most chink beads, chinks are most commonly used only to seal between log courses, cor-

Acrylic Latex Sealants

Note: The following are generalizations and not universally true of all acrylic latex sealants. Some "acrylics" are based on low-quality acrylic polymers or are heavily blended with non-acrylic polymers—which reduces the overall performance. **Note:** An acrylic latex product that is "siliconized" may or may not actually perform better than one not making such a claim—sometimes such claims are merely marketing hype. **Note:** Virtually all chinking products are made from acrylic latex.

Pros	Cons
Water cleanup	Sensitive to moisture until cured—can wash out before curing is completed
Low odor	In cold weather should be tented and initially kept warm
Low toxicity	Can take several days (or even weeks) to fully cure, depending on bead size and weather (especially if cool/cold and humid)
Extremely easy to apply, tool, and work with (overall, the best to work with)	Cures worst in cold/cool, wet/humid weather
Non-flammable	Lower performing brands often cannot handle as much movement as most solvent-based or reactive type of sealants
Very good or excellent adhesion to wood and most common surfaces	Can freeze solid, and must be completely thawed out before being used.
Excellent resistance to weathering—resists UV light and oxidation very well	Some types not freeze-thaw stable and cannot be package-frozen before use
Almost always meets the environmental regs. In all jurisdictions—nationwide	Some shrinkage, but not severe
Easily paintable/stainable with latex and oil-based coatings	
Excellent flexibility and elasticity	
Modest in cost, compared to other polymer systems	
Can be applied to damp surfaces—but not when surfaces are actively wet	
Cures best in warm, dry weather	
Fresh material typically adheres well to old dried material of the same kind	

Polyurethane Sealants

Pros	Cons
Usable in most weather conditions—usable when cool and wet (but must be applied to dry surfaces—not rain damageable)	Often contains low levels of isocyanates—with toxicity and sensitizing effects—which can be severe for some people
Excellent adhesion to wood and most surfaces	Typically a very bad odor—best to be used only on the exterior
Good to excellent flexibility and elasticity	Often sticky and difficult to tool and work with
Accepts virtually all latex or oil-based coatings well	Cleans up only with solvents
Fresh material typically adheres well to old dried material of the same kind	1-part types can take several days (or even weeks) to cure—depending on bead size and weather (especially when cold and low humidity or dry)
2-part versions can completely cure in a matter of a few hours—in virtually all weather conditions	Can be very hard to apply in cold weather because the product is thick and pasty when cold (should be kept warm until just prior to being used)
Good to excellent resistance to weathering	Often contains solvents—with potential toxicity and flammability hazards
Cures best in warm, humid weather	1-part versions (the most common) cure worst in cold, dry weather
Overall, can be a good choice for log homes, but the precautions of this listing should be carefully taken into account	Occasionally, the adhesion can be so high and the modulus also high that substrate failure can occur—the worst and most expensive type of failure
All types are freeze-thaw stable in the package (Note: The overall, long-term package stability of 1-part urethanes is not good—often curing out in the tube)	Have little ability to "stress relax" when under tension—never lessening the force applied to the sealant or the bondline when flexed
Minimal shrinkage	1-part types packaged in non-plastic tubes, therefore not very rugged

Silicone Sealants

Pros	Cons
Most weather-resistant chemistry that is readily available	Typically, silicones have poor adhesion to wood (especially in wet conditions)
Easily gunnable at virtually all temperatures—even down to or below zero	Typically will not readily accept paint or stain (the "paintable" versions typically aren't very paintable/stainable and do not perform as well as the non-paintables)
Usable in most weather conditions—with better curing properties than urethanes	The silicone oil plasticizers used in most sealants can migrate to adjoining surfaces and prevent those from being coatable or sealable
Relatively low in toxicity to work with—much better than polyurethanes	Sometimes new silicone will not adhere to old, cured silicone—making repair difficult and expensive
All types are freeze-thaw stable in the package	Many silicones are sticky and stringy to tool and work with
Minimal shrinkage	Many silicones have a strong acid odor (smelling like strong vinegar)
	Overall, not a good choice for the log home industry
	Most types are fragile—tearing easily (unzipping) if slightly cut and stressed
	Little ability to "stress relax"—never lessening the stress on the bondline/sealant

Figure 3–7. Sealing comparison charts.

Synthetic Rubber, Solvent-Based Sealants

Pros	Cons
All weather application—but should be kept warm until just prior to use for easier gunning	Contains solvents that are hazardous and flammable—however, usually a lower health risk than being exposed to isocyanates
Many are crystal clear—the clearest sealants readily available	Sticky and difficult to tool
Excellent adhesion to wood and virtually all surfaces	Should be applied to dry surfaces
Very good weatherability	Bad odor—best used on the exterior (but odor typically
Readily accepts latex paints/stains right away and oil-based coatings within a week and, unlike silicones, does not cause adhesion problems of coatings on adjoining surfaces (because there is no plasticizer "bleed")	dissipates fairly quickly)
	Cleans up only with solvents
	Significant shrinkage—due to solvent evaporation
Fresh material typically adheres to old, dried material of the same kind—making repair easy and relatively inexpensive	
Readily cures in all types of weather—no real limitations	
Good to excellent flexibility and elasticity	
Overall, a good choice for the log home industry when weather conditions require the use of all-weather sealant	
All types are freeze-thaw stable in the package	

Butyl Sealants

Pros	Cons
Excellent adhesion to wood and all other surfaces	Little or no elastic properties—stretches like chewing gum, but has no elastic recovery (readily fails when used in expansion/contraction joints)
Once dried, accepts latex and oil-based stains and paints	
Very good to excellent weatherability	
The most water repellent sealant known	Usable only where there is little or no expansion or contraction of the joint
All weather application—but guns easier if kept warm until just prior to use	Extremely sticky and messy to apply and tool—with "cob-webbing" a major problem (perhaps the messiest sealant there is to work with)
The best use is in "shear" joints—like between sheet metal used in HVAC, gutters, roof flashing, etc (in such uses, butyl is the best)	
	Solvent cleanup
All types are freeze-thaw stable in the package	Solvent odor
	Overall, not appropriate for most applications on log homes

Oil-Based Sealants

Pros	Cons
Excellent adhesion to wood and most all other substrates	Most versions ultimately cure hard as a rock, others stay "chewy" for a long period of time but have little or no elastic properties
Immediately resistant to rain	
All weather application—but guns easier if kept warm until just prior to use	Solvent cleanup required
Moderate to good weatherability	Some can contain enough solvent to be considered combustible
All types are freeze-thaw stable in the package	Sticky to tool—but not as bad as some other types of sealants
Once dried, accepts latex and oil-based stains and paints	Overall, not a good choice for log homes—due to poor movement capability
Cheap—generally, the cheapest available	Can take several days or even weeks to cure (depending on bead size and weather)

Polysulfide Sealants

Pros	Cons
All weather application—but guns easier if kept warm until just prior to use	Not readily available through most channels of distribution—an industrial product
The best chemical resistance of all major types of sealants	Odor not very good (sulphur smell)—should be used only on the exterior
Excellent adhesion to wood and most substrates—including itself	
2-part versions completely cure in a few hours	Some contain solvents—hazardous and combustible
Immediately resistant to rain	Can be sticky and difficult to tool and work with
Very good to excellent weatherability	1-part versions can take days or weeks to cure (in cold, dry weather)
All types are freeze-thaw stable in the package	
Once dried, accepts latex and oil-based stains and paints	Can be a little more expensive than polyurethanes—comparable to silicones
Excellent elasticity and flexibility	
Overall, a good choice for the log home industry	
Minimal shrinkage	

Figure 3–7. Continued. (Courtesy: Sashco)

ners, and around beams. Chink applications are generally used in conjunction with caulks. In this case, caulks are used to seal around windows, doors, checks, cracks, and any other place you don't want a

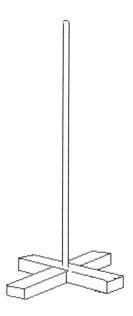

Backer Rod Spool Holder

conspicuous bead. Once you have decided on a sealant, you will want to design a "proper bead." In addition to weather considerations, a proper bead incorporates the use of backer rod.

Backer Rod

A properly designed bead joint for both caulks and chinks calls for "two point adhesion." You will achieve maximum elasticity and flexibility when the sealant adheres to the top and bottom of the joint, not the middle. Do this by packing the joint with backer rod prior to applying the sealant. These joints include (a) seams between log courses, (b) purlin or rafter connections to log walls, (c) corner log intersections, (d) post connections, (e) checks and cracks, and (f) any wide gap requiring the application of sealant—in other words, seams or gaps created by log to log, or log to framing/trimwork connections. Stuff the gaps with a putty knife and, if necessary, secure with either staples or a small dab of caulk. Using a cheap plastic putty knife after sanding the leading edge and corners to be more rounded works well. Backer rod is an insulating type material that is very pliable and comes in varying sizes and lengths. The two main types are defined as *open cell* and *closed cell*. Both types are made of very resilient materials and as such have excellent "memories." If used correctly, they will both expand and con-

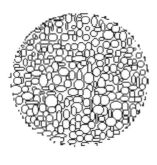

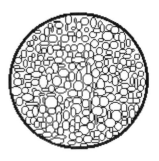

Open Cell

Closed Cell

tract with log movement. The most popular available shape is round. However, other shapes are available. They include half round, triangular, and trapezoidal.

Open Cell

Open cell backer rod is a flexible, round polyurethane product. This product compresses more than the closed cell and is identified by its cream color and spongelike appearance. Primarily, the open cell characteristic allows for airflow so that the sealant cures faster. Also, because of its structure, no air bubbles or pinholes in the sealant will occur. While the material looks and feels like a sponge, in the words of the manufacturer: "However, open cell structure (polyurethane) does not absorb any more moisture than closed cell (polyethylene). The open cell gives you approximately 4 times more surface area per linear foot. If moisture enters the joint, it has more surface area to cling to. It is not, I repeat, it is not absorbed." In spite of this information, I use open cell backer rod on interior joints only.

Closed Cell

Closed cell backer rod is an extruded polyethylene product. Known by its black color and availability in round or trapezoidal shapes, closed cell backer rod is used mainly in exterior joints because it is more rigid. Care has to be taken not to rupture the material when packing it into log joints. If it is, *outgassing* occurs. Outgassing is the formation of air bubbles or pin holes on the surface of the sealant as the gases escape. Once the gases from the ruptured cells escape, outgassing is no longer a problem. Obviously, the bubbles and pin holes are a weakness in the finished bead and must be worked out. Because log home sealants "skin over" relatively quickly, the best remediation is removing and then reapplying the sealant in the affected area. So, why would you use a closed cell backer rod? It is a firmer material than the open cell, allowing for a smoother-looking finished bead.

Regardless of the type you choose, both come in a variety of sizes and lengths.

Open Cell	Closed Cell
3/8"–2"	$^1/_4$"–4"

The extrusion process allows the closed cell to be offered in a single length, coiled around a spool. To aid in working with this material, a jig made out of a broom handle and two two by fours works well. After placing the spools on the broom handle, place the stand on the ground, stuff the starting end of the backer rod in your pocket, and reel off the length needed.

Here is a rule of thumb when you need multiple sizes of backer rod: Measure the widths of the largest and smallest gaps to be filled. Choose a backer rod ¼ " larger than both. Estimate total lengths for both sizes. Then add 10 percent. In addition to large and small sizes, intermediate sizes are usually needed. If you use open cell material, choose one to two intermediate sizes; closed cell, choose two to three intermediate sizes. Estimate the intermediate lengths at 25 percent of the total lengths needed.

See the section on "Applying Chink" later in this chapter for additional tips.

Applying the Sealant

Before going to the store to buy materials and tools, spend a few minutes here. Sealant materials are generally sold in five-gallon pails, thirty-ounce tubes, and ten-ounce tubes. Which one do you get? The most economical by quantity is the five-gallon pail. But, you will also need two bulk loading guns along with nozzles and tips and a gun-loading mechanism. One gun would be the larger thirty-ounce size for general application, and the other gun a ten-ounce size for the hard to reach areas. Nozzles and tips are available in a variety of shapes and sizes, are interchangeable, and are great for consistency. The gun-loading mechanism is meant to ease the process of loading your gun and keeps the threads clean when the nozzle is put back on. These items are expensive, so unless you want to spend the money, this may not be an option. For home owner applications, I generally recommend the thirty-ounce and ten-ounce cartridge tubes supplied in ten-tube cartons. Make sure to get both sizes because you'll need both. A rule of thumb I use is for every four cases of thirty-ounce tubes, order one case of ten-ounce tubes.

Next, are the cartridge-type caulk guns. Get good quality guns. Your hand will thank you before the first day is done. I find the notched ratchet-action guns to be the most user-friendly, especially during cooler weather.

The viscosity of the material at that time requires more trigger pressure. The friction-ratchet guns require more trigger force, even during warmer weather, so I don't like to use them. The nicer guns have tip cutting and puncturing tools attached. When it is time to cut the tip, here are some hints:

1. When preparing to run beads, cut the tip on two tubes. One tube will be for running beads along the seam between courses and corners, the other for filling larger gaps.

2. On the tube for running beads along the seams, cut the tip at a slight angle no larger than three-quarters the size of your desired finished bead.

3. On the tube for filling larger gaps, cut the tip straight and as much as you want.

4. If they are not cut right the first time, don't worry. You will find out fast what works best for you.

You will also need a couple of spray bottles, a $1^1/_2$-inch-wide putty knife, "tooling" tools, a bucket for water and rags, and a five-gallon empty pail. Denatured alcohol and a length of clear plastic tubing may also be needed; these are covered in the next section on "Applying Caulk."

Use the spray bottle when the bead is ready to be tooled. Poly-foam brushes are great for tooling, but you might want to use a pastry brush, small metal spatula, popsicle sticks, or just your finger. Don't confuse poly-foam with foam brushes. Foam brushes will not hold up as well as poly-foam. To figure the quantity of poly-foam brushes:

1. Divide the lineal feet of log in your house by 300.

2. Multiply that by 4.

3. The answer is the number of brushes you will probably go through.

A one-gallon pail works well for the water used to clean off the surface after tooling, and especially if tooling is done with a finger. Make sure to constantly change the water. Clean water will leave a better appearing finished bead. The time to change water is when a lot of sealant grit settles in the bottom of the pail. The best material to use for rags is one like the hand towel you find on a roll in places like gas station rest rooms. Leftover rolls can be purchased from a local linen service. The important features are that they are soft, absorbent, and all cotton. Try not to reuse the rays after you have used them for one day.

The five-gallon pail serves as a receptacle for tools, extra rags, brushes, extra caulk tubes, and trash.

Note: I have included my own worksheet for figuring quantities at the back of the book. If it works for you, copy it and use it.

Weather Considerations

Just as we are concerned with exposure to direct sunlight in the application of finishes, we also are concerned with exposure to sunlight in the application of sealants. I have applied sealants in a greater range of log surface temperatures, but most manufacturers suggest the same application range as those for finishes. Like finishes, it is wise to apply the sealant on shaded walls first and work around the structure as the sun moves. Depending on the size of the finished bead, time needs to pass until the sealant "skins over" and cures sufficiently so as not to be affected by rain. Cover your work with plastic if rain or a heavy dew is forecasted. *Do not* let a recently finished bead get wet and run down the wall. Not only is a water-run bead ugly, but it is a pain to clean up and repair. If the work needs to be covered with plastic, the best approach is to cover the entire wall up to the soffit. That way water runoff will not get behind the plastic and run down the wall. Make sure to allow for sufficient airflow from side to side, and keep the area covered until the rain stops or the material has developed enough of a skin to be impervious to water.

Applying Caulk

With a whisk broom, brush off the surface the caulk will be applied to. Blowing off the surface with compressed air works also. The cleaner the surface, the better the application.

It is easier to caulk one feature at a time. I usually do the features in this order:

1. wall log checks
2. intersecting corners

Interior caulking beads showing: (1) before applying a finish, (2) after applying a finish, (3) how well a caulk bead can be hidden by matching the caulk color and finish color. Incidentally, even though these beads are small, they were run four years ago and still show no sign of stress.

3. around windows and doors
4. seams between log courses
5. posts

Doing one feature at a time keeps the job methodical, and it is done more completely and consistently.

The secret to a professional-looking bead is to never run a bead using more material than needed. Run a short section first, tool it, and move on. Get used to the process. Until you get used to running beads, using less is fine. Using more is not only a waste of material, it is but harder to clean up.

Checks

After packing backer rod, work the log checks first, running a bead through the entire check and leaving a "mound" effect in the middle. Try to run material to the edges, but not over the edges. You will find as you are running beads that you will leave ridges and waves in your run because pressure on the gun trigger and the motion you use to lay the bead down. Try to keep these to a minimum. The more the initial bead looks like your finished bead, the less tooling you will have to do.

Next, spray the entire run with water. Watch how fast the water evaporates. You will want the water to stay on the surface of your bead until you are done tooling it. If it evaporates too fast and the sealant skins over before you can tool it, keep spraying the bead, or move to a more shaded wall. Another trick is to add denatured alcohol to the water. The faster the water evaporates from an untooled bead, the more alcohol that is added. I generally use alcohol only toward the end of the job, when there are no more shaded sections to move to.

When tooling the bead, take the chosen tool and get it wet. Pat the material into the gap and toward the ends of the check, using several small strokes. The objective is to push the material into the gap for better sealing. Do not push too hard as this will push material on to your tool, leaving clumps along the edge of the check. When done patting the material in, rinse the tool off in the water bucket and spray the material again. With long, soft strokes, "paint" the material to finish the edges and smooth the appearance. Keeping the tool wet should remove any accidental clumps and leave a clean edge on the run. If, after tooling, the finished bead looks messy, try scraping the edges with the putty knife and wiping the edges down with a wet rag. When deciding which checks to fill, this simple rule should help: Fill anything a quarter-inch or wider, especially those on the upper curvature of the logs. Smaller checks on the upper curvature can be filled, too, but the finish material should fill a majority of them.

The reason for the mound effect is twofold:

1. As the material cures and moisture evaporates, what is left over will be flush with the surface of the log, allowing for better runoff.
2. There needs to be sufficient material in the check to allow for flexibility and elasticity, lessening the chance for material failure.

Don't worry about pressing the material in so that the concave of the hourglass effect is achieved. The important features are: (a) adhesion to the top and bottom surfaces and, (b) enough sealant material to allow for log movement.

Corners

Moving on to the corners and other log intersections, try to work for the same mound effect. Tooling here becomes a little trickier because of the radius of the logs. This is the main reason for doing one feature at a time. Get used to the motion needed to achieve the right finished bead; it will become easier the more you do it. To run the right bead in this situation, you will need a more fluid motion and consistency in running the bead. Start at an intersection where a course seam meets a corner seam and squeeze out a little extra material before running the radius. With as fluid a motion as you can muster, run a bead that follows the radius to the next intersection and finish by squeezing out extra material. As you run the radius, change the direction of the tip so that the point follows the seam. The objective is to fill the gap and leave as much wood exposed as possible. With experience, you can probably run several courses before starting to tool. There are two reasons for the extra material at the corner intersections: It will give a more finished look, and this is where most of the weather infiltration gaps occur.

Tool this run the same way as you did the checks. Spray the material, pat the material into the seam, and smooth out for the finished bead. Smooth out the bead by using the edge of the brush. When done, spray the entire run to remove any excess or leftover grit. Because the material will remain spongy for a while, run a short section of the straight seam at this time to avoid tool prints in the corner.

Windows and Doors

When caulking around windows and doors, it is imperative to seal the entire unit *completely*. Starting at the top, work down one side, then the other, then the bottom. Make sure to leave no gaps in the application, as these become sources of water infiltration. Also, caulk the joints between the pieces of trim. If you decide to apply chink to a structure, try caulk around windows and doors. Otherwise, the wider chink application can become too busy when viewed from far away. For the most effective application, remember that at least a half-inch bead is needed.

Course Seams

You will decide the width of the straight seam bead between courses based on how much additional shrinking and swelling you expect out of the logs. If the logs are green, over 19 percent moisture content, wait a season. Or, if you want a wider bead, run the beads then. A rule of thumb is that the bead should be four times the anticipated log movement. (See the section on "Moisture, Humidity, and Movement" in Chapter 1 for a discussion on seasonal log movement.) Course seam beads are the easiest beads to run and tool. Because these are also the first item spotted for finished appearance, they should be clean and neat. Once you decide on the finished bead width, cut the tip on the tubes to about three-quarters the size of the finished bead. Cut the tip at a slight angle. To achieve a consistent bead, try this tip. Rest the pinky, ring, and middle fingers of the hand that will hold the gun on the log just under where the bead will be run. Rest the gun on your hand with the tip lightly touching the logs and centered over the seam. Now, rotate the tube in the gun so that the point on the tip *follows* the seam in the direction the bead will run. Next, angle the gun so that the angle cut at the tip runs parallel with the log surface. As the bead is run, your hand will serve to steady the run as long as you keep those three fingers moving along the length of the log. Consistent pressure on the trigger will reduce the ridges and produce a smooth bead. With experience, you may find that a fluid motion is easier to maintain if you start the run by leaning to the left or right and shift your weight as you move in the opposite direction. The key here is to keep the gun in the same position relative to the seam being run. Finally, watch the material as it comes out. The speed of laying a run is dictated by the amount of material being applied. Start slow with little pressure and don't allow the material to squeeze around the tip. Don't go too fast either, otherwise a string will run out. The best speed is where the material just starts to form a ridge or wave beyond the point of the tip.

Tooling is the same. Spray the material, lightly pat the material into the seam, and with a wet brush, smooth it out lightly. Use long, even strokes for best results. When done, spray the bead again to allow loose material and grit to run off.

Posts

When sealing posts, use a combination of the techniques described above.

Hard-to-reach places include the plate log to soffit connection, purlin to soffit connection, behind a framed wall, and so forth. Running a bead is one problem; tooling them is another. Use the half-inch clear plastic tubing here. Cut an appropriate length for the application. Place this tubing over the tip of the caulk tube and then place the tubing on the seam to seal. For tooling, try an unwound wire coat hanger with a small rag tied in a ball.

Applying Chink

The preparations for chinking are the same as for caulking, with one exception. To get the maximum flexibility and elasticity out of the material, lay backer rod down before running the chink bead. This concept is called "two point adhesion," and it is explained in the section on backer rod earlier in this chapter. The principle behind this is that maximum elasticity is attained when sufficient material is laid down and bonds to the top and bottom surfaces only. Backer rod serves as a "bond breaker" by not allowing the chink material to bond to the backside of the joint. In addition, chink material will not bond to the backer rod, which leaves the material adhering only to the top and bottom of the joint.

The size of backer rod depends on the size of the finished bead and the radius of the logs. Generally speaking, divide the finished bead size by four if round backer rod material is used; divide by two if flat material is used, such as Grip-strip.

When applying backer rod or Grip-strip, attach it to the log surface. Usually, compressing backer rod into the seam to be chinked is sufficient. However, sometimes you may need to use a stapler. I use an air-powered stapler. A dab of caulk or adhesive also works. You do not want to be fighting the material falling out of the joint while you are applying the chink.

The tools you'll need for tooling are the same as those for caulking. I have used a lot of different tools, but I have found the poly-foam brush to be the best. The size to purchase should be the size of the finished bead. I also use a bulk gun exclusively for chinking because of the wide assortment of tips and the control needed when running a bead. If the finished beads are going to be in the 1 to $1^1/_2$-inch range, the thirty-ounce and ten-ounce cartridge tubes will work fine. However, if the finished bead is going to be in excess of 2 inches, the bulk guns will save time, money, and aggravation.

When preparing the cartridge tube, cut the tip at a shallower angle than you would with the caulk tubes and about three-quarters the diameter of the finished bead. The difficulty with running a chink bead is the sheer mass of material. It takes a bit of practice, so try running and tooling beads on scrap material first. Running beads without the ridges (see "Applying Caulk" earlier in this chapter) is also important. However, because of the size of these beads, the ridges are easier to work out than they are with caulks. The ridges can be used as an indication of applying the right amount of material. Finally, depending on what the final tooled bead is to look like, the initial run should match that appearance as close as possible so that tooling is kept to a minimum. Here, the three-finger run works extremely well.

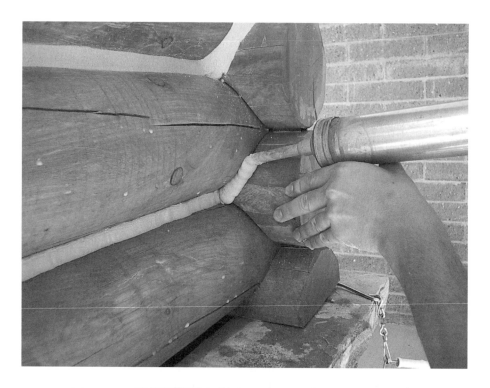

The above pictures show the running of the chink bead: 1) balancing the gun and using fingers as a guide; 2) spray enough water to keep the bead moist while tooling; 3) tooling for smooth lines and an even texture; 4) a recently completed bead that is still wet. After tooling, spray the bead to remove loose bead material. When it dries, the wet streaks will disappear.

Tooling is accomplished the same as with caulking. Spray the bead with water and gently pat the material into the seam. Keep the material wet with a constant spray. While smoothing the bead out, keep the brush wet and brush the bead gently with long, even strokes. There will be streaks of gritty material running down the wall, but don't worry. These streaks will wash off when the material dries.

Use the same methods for running chink beads around purlins, posts, and log corners as you did for caulk.

Overall, I have found keeping a wet surface on the chink beads until I was done tooling allowed for the most clean, consistent, finished bead.

A word of caution: Since it will take the chink about two weeks to completely cure, someone will invariably want to test the curing of the beads by sticking their fingers in them. If that is going to be an issue, post a scrap piece of plywood in a conspicuous spot and run a short bead at the beginning of every day. Label the beads for the day they were run and direct anyone who wants to test the beads, to stick their fingers in there.

A Proper Bead

As seen in these diagrams, a properly designed sealant bead forms an hourglass effect. You can achieve this by tooling a smooth and flat or slightly convex-shaped bead. As the sealant cures, this shape remains. Remember to leave at least a quarter-inch minimum thickness at the center of the finished bead. Notice the size of backer rod is chosen so that complete compression is avoided. The backer rod should fit snugly with no more than 50 percent compression. Finally, be prepared to check your work after one season. A reapplication is usually necessary because it is virtually impossible to run a consistent, effective bead throughout the entire sealing process. Additional applications are covered in Chapter 4. Another reason for the design and application of a proper bead is energy, or thermal efficiency.

Energy Efficiency

We have all heard the familiar cry about the energy efficiency of log homes. It takes less energy to cool them in the summer and heat them in the winter. Ask a log home manufacturer why and the answer will probably be, "the mass of a solid log." That makes sense, so most of us

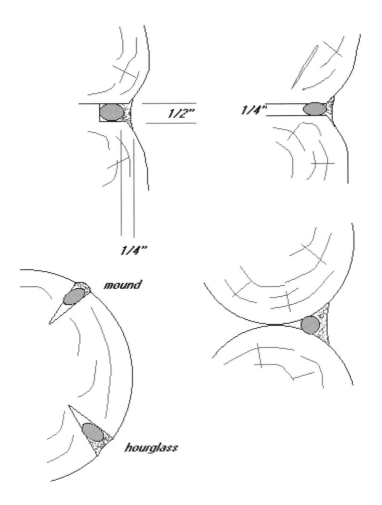

1/2"

1/4"

1/4"

mound

hourglass

are happy. However, consider this: R-value, or resistance value, is a number attained through controlled environment testing measuring a material's resistance to heat conductivity or transmission. To make this more clear, look at it this way. Like a magnet, heat is attracted to cold. Heat always flows to cold. Sometimes, though, heat has to flow through a material to reach cold. R-value is a measure of that material's ability to slow the flow. The higher the R-value, the better the material is at restricting the flow.

The average log used in log homes is considered to have an R-value of 1.25 per inch. In other words, for an average 8-inch thick wall log, the equivalent R-value is around 10. Compared to a stick frame wall of the same thickness and with an R-value around 19 to 20, log homes should be energy *inefficient*. But they are not. Test results from a study conducted by the National Bureau of Standards and Department of Energy in 1981 point this out. Why is that? The answer has to do with the thermal mass of logs. Logs have a high capacity for storing heat energy.

Today, *mass enhanced R-value* is the more appropriate measure of the energy efficiency in log homes. But that is only part of the story. Mass enhanced R-value evaluation was studied at the Oak Ridge National Laboratory in 1991. In 1996 a method was established to measure the dynamics of this phenomenon. Before that, thermal mass and energy efficiency of log homes was studied in the late 1970s and early 1980s when the log home industry contracted with Steven Winter & Associates and participated in the National Bureau of Standards and Department of Energy study.

Basically put, heat flow is restricted by the building materials used in walls. Because a log wall has a higher thermal mass than a stick-frame wall, heat flow is slowed down. As the outside air temperature passes through the level of the inside home temperature, heat flow will go out or in. In other words, if the outside temperature is higher than the temperature on the inside, heat will flow in. Conversely, when the outside temperature is lower than the inside temperature, heat will flow out. The mass of logs slows this process down by storing heat as it flows through and passing off, toward the cold, excess heat it doesn't have the capacity to store. The benefits of this process are seen when daily temperature fluctuations are above *and* below inside temperatures.

The energy efficiency of log homes is achieved if a log home is maintained at a constant 68°F inside, and the outside temperatures fluctuate between, say, 45°F and 90°F. If outside air temperatures are either above or below inside temperatures for an extended period, such as during summer and winter seasons, mass enhanced R-value testing points to the efficiencies being lost until the former situation is re-established.

Now, a very important part of a log wall is the sealing system. The question is, does a sealing system affect the energy efficiency of a log home? The answer is, most definitely. According to a test sanctioned by Sashco Sealants and conducted by David McGrew of DPM Energy Research, a properly sealed log home uses high-quality log home specific sealants, which "provide thermal resistance comparable to the logs they join."

Chapter 4

Regular Maintenance

In this section we will discuss general log component inspection and the reapplication of log coating and sealing materials. The difference between regular maintenance and initial maintenance is that a record of maintenance exists, and the steps for initial maintenance have already been performed. Start with an inspection of the log components.

General Log Component Inspection

The main concern here is determining when and if it is time to reapply or touch up coating and sealing materials. This inspection also

includes looking for problems. If this is the first inspection, it should be thorough. (See the section on "Existing Home Inspection" in Chapter 2.) Otherwise, hook up the garden hose and gather a step ladder, extension ladder, scratch awl, and bleach for this process.

Finish Condition

Are there spots where the coating has worn off? Has the upper curvature of each course weathered more than the bottom? Are all exposed log ends still coated? Are there any discolored spots? When was the last time this coating was applied?

The finish condition inspection checks the severity of weathering that the logs have been exposed to. Spots that show a worn finish are a sign of one or more of the following:

> normal wear and weathering patterns
>
> inappropriate material used
>
> prior coat that was too thin
>
> log moisture leaching to and through the surface

The upper curvature of round logs will naturally weather faster than the bottom. This is found on walls with more exposure to weather. Consider coating these sections more frequently. A heavier single coat is not necessarily the answer to this problem. Find out more about this in Chapter 5.

Because of the longitudinal alignment of wood fibers, exposed log ends tend to soak up finishes faster and deeper than log faces. These ends are like a sponge, and just as they can soak up, they can leach moisture, finishes, and preservatives out, too. Exposed log ends need the most attention in the maintenance cycle.

Discoloration could be caused by dirt buildup, splash back, or mold and mildew. Discolorations near the bottom of a log wall are usually dirt buildup or splash back. In this case, wipe the dirt off. If unsure of the discoloration, try a drop of bleach from an eye dropper on the stain. If it turns white, mold or mildew is the most likely culprit. Cleaning the logs with a bleach solution is covered in Chapter 3.

The timing for the last application can be important because if it was done within the past couple of years, an ineffective finish may be the cause. Always, always use the best affordable finish. Here's a lesson in economics. The cost difference between a finish coating that will last five years and a finish coating that lasts two years is negligible. Make the choice of finish decision based on time effectiveness, not cost.

Also, check the finish on the window and door trim, fascia, and soffit for wear. These areas are usually more problematic than log components. Finish touch-ups are covered later in this chapter.

Sealant Condition

The first inspection for sealant application should be done after one heating season has passed. It is unusual to have an initial application done completely and adequately the first time around. Due to the nature of applying this material, inspection is necessary to find the weak spots. Is the sealant still adhering to both log surfaces (top and bottom)? Are there any cohesion failures? Has the sealant bubbled? Have checks opened up, resulting in a need for more sealant? Is the material "chalking"? Chalking is a condition where the sealant material is breaking down, usually because of aging, and has become ineffective. This is also found if less expensive and inappropriate materials have been used.

The problem areas for sealants are usually found on the walls exposed to more sunlight and weather; around all windows, doors and butt joints; and on exposed log ends. In other words, any place where moisture can accumulate and seep into the structure can be a problem area.

Adhesion and cohesion failures are usually caused by:

excessive log movement

normal aging pattern of older sealant materials

wrong sealant materials used for the application

an inadequate amount of sealant material used

incompatibility with finish coating system

If excessive log movement is being experienced, chances are the logs have not dried completely to the ambient or equilibrium moisture level. Initial applications are usually applied between two months and one year after construction begins. Reaching ambient moisture levels can sometimes take up to two years. Your choice then is to wait, test the logs for moisture content, or reapply the sealant material.

I inspected a house once and found that four different types of caulk had been used. Sealant failure was guaranteed in this case. Using the right materials and compatibility are big issues. The two main components for protecting your logs and sealing your home against the weather are the finish and the sealant. Using the right and compatible components are the secrets to a long-lasting finish.

Applying the sealant is all handwork. Consistency is the key. When an entire structure is being done, it is impossible to run consistent beads throughout. That's why it's important to do an inspection to find the weak spots after one heating season has passed. If the initial job was done right, there will not be many of these spots and reapplication will be easier. The good news is, once the initial inspection and reapplication is completed and found to be satisfactory, future inspections should require substantially fewer reapplications.

Component Integrity

This inspection covers signs of decay and excessive weathering. With a scratch awl, look for these signs:

> water stains from runoff
>
> excessive checking on log surfaces and log ends
>
> fresh boring or exit holes from insects
>
> areas of cracks formed like wrinkled aluminum foil
>
> loose pieces of wood on log surfaces

Water stains are signs that water is seeping beneath the coating surface. Because coatings are meant to be water repellents, they also serve to hold moisture in. These surfaces will have to be sanded to remove the coating, bleached to remove the stain, preserved, and recoated. Excessive checking is a sign the logs are drying out more and allowing moisture in. This condition exists mostly on log ends, which need more attention anyway. Depending on the severity of the condition, consider a slurry mix of caulking at best, or an epoxy treatment to completely seal the log ends.

Fresh boring holes are signs the log was previously infected or the log is getting wet and not having the opportunity to dry out. A previously infected log is not necessarily a bad sign. It could be that insect eggs have hatched and the larvae are looking to escape. If the logs were treated with a borate preservative, signs of insects should not be a problem, but you may see these signs for a couple of years. Danger of reinfestation is low. See the section on "Insect Damage" in Chapter 5 for more details.

Crackling on logs is a sign of brown or dry rot and can be a potentially damaging condition. Remediation is generally drilling a series of holes, injecting the area with a borate preservative, and plugging the holes. Depending on the severity of the dry rot, other measures may need to be taken. Caught early, rot is not a structural issue. See the section on "Rot and Decay" in Chapter 5 for more information.

Loose pieces of wood on log surfaces are usually caused by outside forces, that is, someone hitting the log with a sharp or blunt object. Before taking the loose piece out completely, ask yourself, *is it big enough that if I get an adhesive behind it, it will hold?* See the section "Loose Wood Repair" in Chapter 6 for more information.

Conducting a general maintenance inspection should not take long. As mentioned earlier, the first general inspection is to determine how the initial job was done and what areas need additional attention. While conducting this inspection, don't be surprised to find some areas needing more attention than others. The structure needs to acclimate to the different components and local environment, so expect additional movement and some form of settling to occur.

Stripping Methods

There are many methods to consider once you have made the decision to strip the existing finish off the logs. Some methods can be applied to the entire structure, while others should be considered for smaller, more stubborn areas. The following methods are the most common stripping methods.

Power Washing

When I power washed my first log home, I thought this was the way to go. The combination of water and detergent cleaned the logs and the customer was happy. The next job was a log home with a solid finish, and the power washer did not penetrate the finish. In addition, the sealant had failed, allowing cascades of water into the home. Even though I had prepped the inside by draping plastic, it still left a mess. Since that time, I apply these rules when deciding to power wash a structure.

1. Power wash only when the logs need to be cleaned, not stripped.
2. Power wash when wood substrate is solid, not weathered.
3. Power wash when the structure is unoccupied.
4. Power wash when you need to rinse off other stripping agents.

Because the pressure setting should be low when washing log surfaces (~1500–2000 PSI), most power washers can do the job. The expense of a decent power washer is in the range of $400 to $2,000 if you want to buy one, or they can be rented. Even though they are easier on the hands, especially in cold weather, I have not found heated power washers to add enough value to be worth the extra expense.

Also, because of the need to move around most structures, I have found gas engine power washers to be more convenient than the electric motor variety. Finally, an inexpensive feature found on most, but not all, power washers is an in-line extension for the application of detergents. This can be a valuable feature.

The benefits of power washing the log home include a clean surface for applying preservatives, stains, and sealants. Also, by allowing moisture to seep into the home, hard-to-find weather leaks are exposed.

Drawbacks to power washing include the need for extensive preparation, draping plastic on inside walls, and covering valuables, and covering outside plants. Also, "fuzzing" will be left on the logs if the pressure was set too high or the detergent was left on too long. Finally, you must allow the logs to dry completely, sometimes for 2 to 3 days, before moving on to the next step.

Media Blasting

The term *media* is a general term used for the various types of materials available to abrasively remove or strip existing finishes or weathering from log components. As can be seen in the accompanying chart, there are many different types of media commercially available. Media blasting is also known as abrasive blasting and is defined as "the process of propelling abrasive particles from a blast machine using the power of compressed air." An excellent booklet on the safe and efficient use of blasting equipment is *Blast Off 2*, which is available from Clemco Industries Corp. The following comments are excerpts from *Blast Off 2*.

Three fundamental components constitute a blasting setup: air compressor, blast machine system, and abrasive. The compressor must produce sufficient air pressure and volume to convey abrasive from the blast machine to the surface. The blast machine must contain the abrasive and meter it into the air stream with as little restriction as possible. The abrasive utilizes the force of the compressed air to achieve the desired effect on the surface. Cleaning takes place as a direct result of how efficiently air moves from the compressor to the surface being blasted. A restriction in just one part reduces the entire system's production rate.

Coating manufacturers and professional organizations test paint systems by applying them over various surface profiles and subjecting them to a wide range of environmental conditions. They have found that coatings require specific profiles to ensure adhesion to and complete protection of the substrate. The profile provides a mechanical method of positive, uniform bonding between the coating and the surface . . . Many coating failures can be traced to the use of

Abrasive Comparison Chart

Material	Mesh Size	Shape	Density lbs/ft³	Mohs	Friability	Initial Cost	No. of Cycles	Per Use Cost	Source	Typical Application
Silica Sand	6–270	☆ ○	100	5.0–6.0	high	low	1	medium	Nat.	Outdoor blast cleaning
Mining Slag	8–80	☆	85–112	7.0–7.5	high	med.	1–2	medium	b-p	Outdoor blast cleaning
Steel Grit	10–325	☆	230	8.0	low	high	200+	medium	mfg.	Removing heavy scale
Steel Shot	8–200	○	280	8.0	low	high	200+	low	mfg.	cleaning, peening
Alum. Oxide	12–325	☆	125	8.0–9.0	med.	high	6–8	medium	mfg.	Cleaning, finishing deburring, etching
Glass Bead	10–400	○	85–90	5.5	med.	med.	8–10	low	mfg.	Cleaning, finishing
Plastic	12–80	☆	45–60	3.0–4.0	low/med.	high	8–10	medium	mfg.	Paint stripping, deflashing, cleaning
Wheat Starch	12–50	☆	90	2.8–3.0	high	high	1	high	b-p	Paint stripping, cleaning
Corn Cob	8–40	☆	35–45	2.0–4.5	med.	low	4–5	low	b-p	Removing paint from delicate surfaces

☆ = Angular ○ = Spherical Nat. = Natural b-p = Byproduct mfg. = Manufactured

Mesh Size - recommended size and holes per inch

Density - weight of material per cubic foot

Mohs - weight hardness, scale 1–10, 1 = soft, 10 = hard

Friability - material's brittleness or its tendency to break into small particles on impact

No. of Cycles - number times material can be reused effectively after per use screening

Per Use Cost - estimated final cost based on friability and number of cycles

Source - process by which material is generated

Source: *Blast Off 2*, Second Edition, Clemco Industries Corp., Copyright 2002, All rights reserved.

Figure 4–1. Abrasive comparison chart.

the wrong abrasive. The best possible equipment cannot compensate for an abrasive that is not designed for the work. Use high quality abrasives intended for blasting.

Blasting can be dangerous for a poorly trained, poorly equipped operator. A blast machine produces a powerful stream of sharp particles that, in addition to cleaning a surface, creates clouds of potentially toxic dust. To prevent a variety of injuries and illness, personal safety equipment is absolutely necessary for blast operators and anyone in the work area.

Here are two more points to keep in mind: First, position the blasting equipment in an area requiring the least amount of moving. When full, the blast machine itself can weigh close to 300 pounds and be cumbersome to move, along with the air and media hoses. The same goes for the blasting media. Media is usually supplied in bags weighing forty to fifty pounds. If the equipment will have to be moved as the job progresses, anticipate the locations and place media at those locations. Whenever possible, extend the length of hoses but try not to exceed 100 feet. Power is lost as the hoses get longer but not as appreciably up to 100 feet. Second, the spray pattern for media blasting is mesh, just like that for spray painting. Try to produce a stroke that is feathered at both ends for overlapping adjacent blasting runs, is at the same angle throughout, and produces a finished surface texture recommended by the finish manufacturer.

The two most common types used in log home restoration are corn cob media and sand media.

Corn Cob Media

Corn cob media is coming into vogue, but it has been used for many years on other applications. This type of stripping is usually more forgiving than sand media. This method is also aggressive enough for log homes and, depending on the technique you've developed, leaves less fuzzing than sandblasting. The blast pot equipment you need for this method is specialized and, therefore, not available at most rental stores. Some lumber stores that specialize in log home products may have the blast pot equipment. The blast pot should have a control valve for the media, a pressure regulator, and a moisture separator. Different nozzle sizes are available for different spray patterns, but the fan nozzle is probably the most popular. In addition you'll need a compressor capable of generating 125 PSI and 185 CFM. That size compressor is currently found only in "tow behind" models.

Here are some other things to keep in mind when blasting corn cob media:

1. This type of blasting, while aggressive, does not require a lot of preparation with regard to the grounds or log structure. Used properly, the material will not pit glass or aluminum.

2. Corn cob media is biodegradable. Extensive amounts of cleanup are not usually necessary.

3. The media must be kept dry before and during use.

4. Corn cob blasting is more forgiving than sandblasting when you need to be a little more aggressive.

5. Don't be too aggressive; corn cobbing can still pit and damage wood and exposed skin.

6. Corn cob media will generate a dustier environment. Although it is not considered hazardous, a self-contained sandblasting hood is recommended. I use my goggles, respirator, and face shield.

7. Most of what I learned about sandblasting applies to corn cob media blasting, too.

Sand Media

This is probably the most common method used to strip off an existing finish. Most rental stores have the necessary equipment, and the media is inexpensive and readily available. On the downside, the dust generated by this method is considered carcinogenic if you don't use the proper protection. This is causing some regulatory agencies to establish rules regarding the use of protective equipment and disposal of used media.

Keep the following in mind when you use this method:

1. Use silica sand that you buy at the lumberyard, not regular sand-box sand. There are usually three available grits: #60—fine, #36—medium, #20—coarse. Choose the appropriate grit for the job you need to accomplish.

2. If you use the medium or coarse grit, go over the structure again with the fine grit. This will give you a better surface for the finish application.

3. Keep the sand dry. Otherwise, it will clog up the nozzle.

4. If you are renting the equipment, get an extra nozzle for the gun.

5. The nozzles are a round ceramic material and wear down fast on this type of job. This is not the best type of nozzle for this type of work, but it is adequate.

6. Sandblasting is very abrasive and aggressive. Use even strokes from a consistent distance, about 10 inches.

7. Be careful around surfaces you do not want sandblasted—windows, trim, aluminum doors for instance. If you are not careful, any of these grits will pit and damage these surfaces.

8. When you encounter a tough spot, whether it has a heavy coating or is hard to reach, sand the spot by hand. Do not get too aggressive.

9. If you haven't done this before, practice on a scrap mock-up. If at all possible, do not practice on your structure unless you are confident you will not damage the wood.

10. For your protection and easier cleanup, wear coveralls, goggles, a respirator, and a hat. Wear a face shield over the goggles and respirator. The sand grit eventually will clog the goggles and respirator, but the face shield will allow you to work longer before you need to clean them.

11. Accumulated piles of sand around the structure need to be vacuumed up and disposed of properly.

12. If the sand has not accumulated any moisture, screen it for reuse. Generally, I do not reuse sand media because it usually takes too long to screen it. Also, the nature of the material is that it basically explodes when it hits the surface being blasted, so all that is left is a finer grit, or dust.

13. Measuring the quantity of sand media needed for a particular job is difficult. When unsure, start with three to five 100-pound bags and see how far that goes. Get used to the process using the first bag; measure the area done with the second bag. Order two or three bags more than you think will be needed.

14. I have found I generally go through twice as much coarser grit on any given structure.

Chemical Stripping

This method requires very close attention and is best left to a professional applicator. There are two types of chemical stripping available: caustic and solvent. Many woodworkers have used one or both methods on smaller scale projects, but they can be used on stripping a log home. Both methods have a proven track record, but I prefer to use them sparingly.

1. Use chemicals in conjunction with other stripping methods, sanding, and blasting.
2. Use chemicals only on very heavy coatings and extremely tough areas.
3. Follow instructions on the containers, *to the letter*.
4. Chemicals will dry or evaporate faster on a warm, sunny day. Mist the chemical with a spray bottle until you are ready to remove it.
5. Chemical stripping is expensive.
6. Most chemicals will darken the wood surface and thus require applying an oxidizing agent.
7. Caustic chemicals are corrosive and acidic and as such need to be neutralized.
8. Oxalic acid is a good neutralizer and oxidizer.
9. To remove any residual chemical when done, always power wash the surface.
10. Chemicals can cause more serious fuzzing of log surfaces, requiring some hand sanding.

Again, use chemicals sparingly and only if necessary. Because regulations are becoming more restrictive regarding their use, disposal can be an expensive problem.

Reapplying Preservatives

In this section we will look at the borate preservatives you can apply. Even though some manufacturers pretreat their wood materials, reapplication of a preservative should not be discounted. Since the focus is on the home owner, there is one class of preservatives that is the undisputed king—borates. These preservatives are colorless and somewhat odorless and will not adversely affect stain applications. In powder or concentrated gel form, they are mixed with water and sprayed, brushed, or rolled on the log surfaces. While there are claims of penetration up to 2 inches, moisture contents have to be in excess of 25 percent to achieve that. Remember, equilibrium moisture content will vary from 6 to 11 percent. As log components dry down to the EMC, borates can leach out of the log during this process. For our purposes, borate penetration is usually no more than three-quarters of an inch. As a result, due to the leaching capability of these preservatives, periodic reapplication is a necessity. For purposes of this discussion, log preservatives should not be confused with water repellents (WRs) or water repellent preservatives (WRPs). The reason for this is these preservatives are not water repellent. Borate preservatives are generally drawn to water. When a preserved log gets wet, the borates will migrate toward the moisture. Since this preservative is near the surface of the log, it can leach out. If the logs stay dry, the borates remain stable. That is why it is important to maintain a water repellent coat over the preservative.

Preservation Research Group provides an excellent discussion on borates:

> These products, when handled and applied according to the directions, are safe and easy to use. Borate based products are not completely new. Reports from the 1940s on through to current research document the efficacy of borates as wood preservative. With recent EPA rulings to remove hazardous formulations from the market, borates are sensible and reliable choices.
>
> Borate products are effective against both wood boring insects and decay fungi. Research has shown that .084 lbs. of borates per cubic foot of wood is sufficient to provide protection against most wood destroying fungi. *[Author's note: Logs properly treated with Penetreat, Timbor, Armor-Guard, or any of the premixed glycol solutions receive a level of up to .25 lbs/cu.ft.]* The fungi can still germinate due to the protective shell of the spores, but the wood is protected since the fungi cannot develop without ingesting fatal levels of borate. The concentrations needed to kill wood boring insects are generally less than the amounts needed to control fungi.
>
> A real advantage to borate based wood treatments is that the borate migrates through the wood and so it is more than just a surface treatment. This means that by selecting the correct product, borate protection can diffuse deeper into the wood, without the need for pressure treatment. Most plywood glue lines (carbamide and PVAC glues) do not prevent the diffusion of borates. In relatively dry conditions, long term protection is expected (20–50 years). Long term exposure to wet conditions can cause the borates to migrate out of the wood. In wet conditions or ground contact, additional applications will be necessary (after 1, 2, 3 or more years depending on conditions). The ability of borates to diffuse makes them well suited for remedial or eradication treatments of moist wood.

Unlike other preservative products, borate products can be applied at the first signs of decay while the wood is still wet. The moisture in the wood will help diffuse the borates through the susceptible area. This can stop the deterioration from advancing and reduce the potential for costly repairs. Sometimes a combination of borate products is needed to provide for both stopping the immediate deterioration and for long term protection.

The use of borate wood protection products has many advantages when considering the remedial and preventative treatment of wood in place: ability to diffuse through wood, low vapor pressure, reasonable cost and relatively low toxicity.

Reapplying Finishes

In this section we will deal with general tips and methods for the reapplication of finish materials. There are many materials available on the market to choose from, all with their own instructions. Read those instructions carefully and use them in conjunction with any of these tips.

The first step is to clean the log surfaces.

Cleaning Log Surfaces

Assuming the existing finish is not experiencing substantial failures, simply spraying down the surfaces with water may be sufficient. A garden hose with a jet spray or a pressure washer works fine for this. If you use a pressure washer, make sure the setting is low, or around 1,000 PSI. If you can reach the entire wall from ground level, the first step is to wet the wall. Pressure is not a consideration. The idea is to get loose particles wet so they will fall off easier during the next step.

Starting at the top of the gable or wall, hold the nozzle about 12 inches from the surface and spray horizontally along the length of the fascia, soffit, and logs. Working methodically down the surface, dirt and other airborne particles should wash off easily. For stubborn areas or areas where the coating is flaking, a stiff-bristle brush works well. Don't be bashful. Use some elbow grease to get all the dirt off the surfaces. For particularly stubborn areas, use a mild detergent (dishwashing soap) and water to clean the surface. Mix it up in a bucket and brush it on. Let it set for a minute or two, brush it in again, and then completely rinse it off.

If someone hasn't yelled from the inside yet because of water running down the wall, go inside and look to see if any of the water is seeping in. If any runs are found, try to track where the water is coming in from and make a note to reseal that area. Do not assume that infiltration is at the point the water is running down the wall. The common places to find water coming in are usually butt joints, checks, knots, and around window and door openings.

Clean the rest of the structure the same way, checking for leakage on those walls, too. When done, let the logs dry completely before continuing with the finish application.

If it is important that the sealant bead accents the finish application, there are three ways to achieve this:

1. Mask off the existing bead.
2. Reapply a thin bead of sealant over the existing bead, after applying the finish.
3. Apply a brushover product once the sealant has been touched up.

In any event, the next step is reapplying the finish.

General Finish Application

Here, the method of reapplication is the same as for the initial application. (See the section on "Finish Application Tips" in Chapter 3.) The

assumption here is the use of the same finish material as before, because a change at this point will require stripping the existing finish off and starting again.

If you saved the Masonite shield, get it out again. If not, take a scrap piece of one-quarter-inch-thick Masonite (or similar material) measuring about 12 inches by 20 inches. On a 12-inch side, cut out a radius matching the log posts. It is not necessary to get the entire diameter, just a concave surface to place around the posts as the finish is being applied. On a 20-inch side, cut out a handle for your hand to fit through.

You'll need to drape drop cloths over shrubbery or other vegetation. Drop cloths are also good protection for porch roofs and other overhangs under a section of log to be recoated. I remember a job where I spent some time covering and protecting the windows and doors. But I didn't cover the valley flashing. The stain finish got sprayed all over the flashing and looked unsightly. After trying several methods to clean the flashing, I ended up having to replace it. So, don't forget to cover anything and everything that shouldn't be recoated.

Covering some surfaces to protect them may require using masking tape. Try using the blue tape. Although it is more expensive, it peels off a lot easier than regular masking tape.

To touch up a small area, try using a rag and daub the area. This reduces the lap marks.

Also, practice before setting out to reapply the finish. I find it helpful every time I start a new job to practice the technique I plan to use in an inconspicuous corner. Try not to use a scrap piece of uncoated wood. This will not give an accurate finished appearance.

Most importantly, regardless of what application technique you choose, don't forget to brush. *Brushing is very important.*

Reapplying Sealants

In this section we will discuss the reapplication of sealant material to repair an existing bead. It is very important to use the same material that was used before. Mixing and matching caulks is not only unsightly and unprofessional looking, but also risks sealant failures and compatibility issues.

Reapplying sealant can be done before or after the coating reapplication, but it is generally done before. Remember, the water repellent properties of most stains, paraffinic oils, and waxes are the main culprits concerning compatibility. Most waxes do not allow a solid bond of sealant to wood. If the sealant is not compatible with the finish, simply apply the sealant before the finish.

If you choose to use your finger for tooling, it will get raw and the fingernail worn even after just one day.

The tools needed for reapplication are the same as for the initial application. Before going any further, read the section on "Applying the Sealant" in Chapter 3 to refamiliarize yourself with the process and tools. You will need the following items:

sealant—caulk or chink material
caulk gun
spray bottle
"tooling" tools
bucket for water
rags
empty bucket

If the job was done right the first time, minor touching up is all that should be needed. For caulk touch-ups, the ten-ounce cartridge tubes work best. The smallest unit for chink material however, is usually the thirty-ounce cartridge tubes.

In addition to these application tools, having the following tools is handy for touch-ups:

poly-foam brushes

utility knife

scratch awl or ice pick

1-inch putty knife or paint scraper

compressed air or whisk brush or both

Disk sander (4-inch orbital using resin-backed disks)

Unlike the initial application, where one component is sealed at a time, inspect and repair every resealed component in one working section at the same time. That way, missing a spot is less apt to happen as you move around the structure.

Sealant Inspection

Assuming a general inspection has already been done, during this phase take a closer look at the sealant bead. The general inspection is designed to uncover problems. By taking a closer look, obvious and not so obvious failures can be repaired more thoroughly. Whether you are looking at checks, corner applications, or seam applications, conduct your inspection the same way. First, look for any obvious gaps, holes, or creases where weather will infiltrate. Second, run the scratch awl across the surface, feeling for soft spots or dips. Probe those areas for a possible adhesion failure.

Sealant Application

You'll need a clean surface to apply the new material to, so try pulling the bead out. Don't try too hard. If the bead is still adhering to the joint, remove only the sealant in the area that needs to be repaired. If there is a gap or hole, cut the sealant out around that area. Scuff up the surface of the surrounding sealant. Apply the new bead, tool it, and spray it using the methods described in Chapter 3. If there has been excessive log movement, the sealant material will be torn or separated in the middle of the bead (cohesion failure). Behind this tear or separation will be a gap. Cut through the bead on the top and bottom the entire length of the failed sealant section until you run into solid material. Remove this section. Again, scuff the sealant on both ends for the new bead. Apply the new bead. Tool it and spray it with water. For soft spots and dips, first look for the reasonable cause. If the cause is not enough material having been applied initially, scuff the surface and apply an overcoat, a light covering. If the surrounding wood feels soft or punky, read Chapter 6.

Once you have the techniques down for the initial application, reapplication is a snap. Make sure to do it in a methodical fashion. Unlike in the initial application, where one component around the structure is sealed at a time, reapplication inspection and resealing is done all components in a wall section at the same time.

Compatibility Issues

I am discussing compatibility issues in this chapter because the use of noncompatible products can lead to other problems. Compatibility is the ability of finishes (stains) and sealants (caulks and chinks) to work together, regardless of their order of application.

As stated earlier, for best adhesion of the sealant, the wood material needs to be clean, dry, and sound. The existence of a finish between the sealant and the wood can diminish the service life of the sealant. This is particularly evident when using chink sealants. These beads are usually wider, covering more wood surface. Applied correctly for two point adhesion, the sealant relies on a tight bond with the log material to do its job. The use of a noncompatible finish, applied before the application of the chink, would be confirmed by adhesion failures of the sealant along the top and bottom edges of the bead. As seen in the chart on moisture-excluding effectiveness, paraffin wax has a high percentage effectiveness when compared to other finishes. However, this happens to be the component in most one-coat finish systems that causes the adhesion problem. Even though compatibility is a larger issue with chink sealants than it is with caulk sealants, it should not be discounted when the choice for a sealant is caulk. Caulks are usually applied in a smaller bead and tooled deeper into the seam than chinks.

When using a finish and sealant produced by the same manufacturer, compatibility issues are addressed in the application instructions. If using a finish and sealant produced by two different manufacturers, call the sealant manufacturer for compatibility testing done on the finish you have chosen.

If testing has not been done, the best course of action is to apply the sealant before the finish. If you have chosen to use a chink sealant, it's probably because of the offsetting appearance of the chink against the finish. In other words, a dark finish with a light chink or a dark chink against a light stain. In this scenario, the stain needs to be applied before the chink. Because of that, compatibility becomes an issue. The only option at this point is to use compatible products.

Another compatibility issue is the application of a new finish over an existing finish. This situation happens more when clear-coat finishes are used, several years have passed between applications, and the home has changed ownership. Noncompatible finishes will not bond. They will peel, blister, and crack, allowing moisture to seep under the new coating and cause its failure. When unsure of the type of finish coating applied to the logs, the best answer is to strip it off and start again. (See Chapter 3.) Looking at this in a different light, if the home needs a new finish and you are unsure of the last finish used, chances are it needs to be cleaned anyway. Why not strip and clean the logs and apply a fresh preservative and finish treatment? The additional cost will be worth it, and most likely justified by the aesthetic appeal and peace of mind that follows.

The final compatibility issue is the application of different sealants. In what I would consider to be one of the most drastic of cases, I was called in on a home with several leaks. The home was built in the mid 1970s, sealed with a caulk from that era, and on its fourth home owner. During that time, caulks had a much shorter service life than the materials available today. The material had obviously been chalking for several years, had turned brittle, and was easy to remove in spots. The home's previous owners had patched spots with silicone caulks and butyl rubber caulks. In turn, the new home owners had tried to apply a fresh sealant over the existing beads and were experiencing failures all over the structure. This was an extreme case, and there was only one course of action—strip it, then replace it. The structure had to be stripped of all caulking, cleaned, and resealed.

This is a labor-intensive job that can be expensive. However, when the benefits of a properly sealed home are weighed in, the expense is justified.

Chapter 5

....

Log Component Problems

Two hundred years ago, a log cabin was shelter from the weather. Its primary purpose was temporary so not much thought had to be given to long-term maintenance. Can you imagine the frontier settler packing up the family to go into town on a horse-drawn wagon to have a conversation about downspouts and the quality of chinks and stains?

Thanks to the popularity of log homes today, the level of knowledge about the maintenance of natural log materials exposed to the weather continues to grow. We know a lot about the growth cycle of wood and its processes. Until recently, our knowledge about the return cycle and protecting against decay focused on more utilitarian uses such as pressure-treated lumber materials. But the market is growing for maintaining natural-looking wood. By understanding the how and why of the decay process, better materials are being developed to slow this process down and sometimes stop it.

Thirty years ago, log homes were bought and sold on the premise they required little maintenance. Keeping out the weather was important. When a leak developed, you patched it. Maintenance done. Today, maintaining a fresh, new, natural look is important, making maintenance a key issue. To do this, the decay process has to be understood. (See Chapter 1.)

Researchers at the Forest Products Laboratory in Madison, Wisconsin, have found that the decay process starts as early as one week on untreated, exposed wood. The discoloration experienced on exposed wood is called *weathering*.

Weathering

Weathering of untreated, exposed wood is a natural process. The process starts as soon as the wood is exposed to sun, wind, and rain. Light-colored woods will darken and dark woods will lighten. Long-term exposure eventually causes all exposed woods to become gray. Weathering is the breaking down or photodegradation of surface wood fibers (see Figure 5–1.). As these fibers break down, wind and rain will

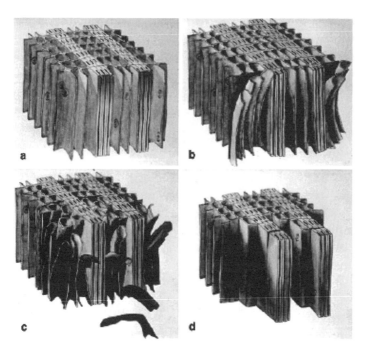

Figure 5–1. Weathering of wood. (a) Unexposed wood; (b) early phase of weather-loosening of fibers; (c) early phase of fiber loss; (d) later phase of weathering-loss of earlywood, leading to "washboard" surface.

Reprinted: *Water Repellents and Water Repellent Preservatives for Wood,* Williams, R. Sam, U.S. Dept. of Agriculture, Forest Service, Forest Products Laboratory, FPL-GTR-109

wash them away in a process called *erosion*. The depth of damage depends on factors such as wood species, growth rate, amount of sunlight exposure, wind, and rain. Because weathering is a slow process and affects the surface to a depth of about a quarter of an inch, by itself it is not considered catastrophic damage. However, erosion opens up the surface structure to penetration of molds, fungi, insects, and moisture. We know these factors cause more severe damage.

The more seriously affected log surfaces are the upper curvature surfaces. These surfaces are exposed to a direct, head-on impact of sunlight rays. At this angle, the upper curvature will experience higher temperatures than even the bottom curvature of the same log, exposing the log to uneven stresses. The higher temperature also causes subsurface moisture to migrate toward the heat, looking for a place to escape, and it may cause whatever finish is used on the logs to blister and fail. The relief of these stresses is seen in the checking and cracking of the wood. Of the different kinds of checks and cracks found in logs, weathering usually leaves small longitudinal cracks spaced closely together. Over time, the appearance and texture of the weathered log surface is rough and uneven with coloring from brown turning to gray.

Remediation of this problem usually means sanding the affected areas or media blasting the entire structure if weathering is extensive.

(See the section on "Media Blasting" in Chapter 4.) Because weathering cracks allow moisture to seep into the substructure, test the logs for core moisture content before applying a finish. Weathering may not be the only problem. By using a resistance-type moisture meter with $2^1/_2$-inch pin leads, find out how much moisture is under the surface of the logs. (See the section "Testing for Moisture Content" in Chapter 1 for more information on moisture meters.) If the moisture content is 15 percent or less, clean the log surface and apply the new finish. If the moisture content is above 15 percent, allow the logs to dry some more before cleaning and applying the new finish.

This is a good time to look at the quality of the finish that will be applied. A good-quality finish, formulated especially for log homes, will offer the best protection and lower the chance of failure. In a heavy weathering situation, penetrating and semipenetrating stains with a high solids content for UV protection are usually recommended.

Also, if evidence of weathering is extreme, look at remedies that will reduce direct exposure to sunlight. These may include adding shade trees, a porch roof, a pergola or perhaps even awnings, or extending the existing roof overhang.

Even though some people like this look, weathered logs do not present a properly prepared surface for finish and sealant application.

A closer look at a log end that has weathered extensively. Notice all the small cracks and checks. An open invitation to all sorts of future (if they haven't already begun) problems.

Rot and Decay

Some repairs are better left to those with experience. In most cases though, experience comes with practice. Experienced applicators can usually perform this type of repair more efficiently and completely. They know what to look for and the causes of different types of decay, and how to remediate the situation.

Regardless of the reason for the decay—insects, fungi, or a combination of both—remediation is the same: Repair the damage, then fix the reason for the damage. Rot does not just happen. There is always a reason for its occurrence. Rot, or decay fungi, is caused by and needs three items to grow: moisture, temperature, and a food source.

By controlling any one of these three items, you will effectively control the spread of rot and decay. For a decay fungi to thrive, the moisture content of the wood component has to be in excess of the fiber saturation point (30 percent moisture content). As previously discussed, this is the easiest item to control. Also, decay fungi grow best when atmospheric temperature is between 50°F and 95°F. Outside

A section of rot where remediation was attempted using the spray on expandable foam. Not a good idea.

these ranges, decay fungi will slow their processes down until they cease activity either below 35°F or above 100°F. By controlling access to the log material, i.e. proper and regular maintenance, you are eliminating the ability of decay fungi to infect the wood. (Refer to the section on "New Construction Design Considerations" in Chapter 2 for a discussion on preventing this type of problem.)

Identification

Even though remediation is the same, it is helpful to understand the different types of decay causing these organisms. Once located and identified, you are better prepared to seek out the cause of moisture and take the necessary steps in preventive maintenance. (Figure 5–2 shows which parts of the United States are prone to greater decay due to climate.) Before we get into the identification of decay fungi, understand there are many forms in each category. We are not concerned with identifying each strain; it is sufficient to discuss only the main categories.

Mildew

Mildew is normally found in high-moisture areas such as bathrooms, laundry rooms, or under the kitchen sink. Colors vary from white to brown, yellow, gray, green, even black. It is usually powdery in texture. Mildew itself does not cause structural damage but it will stain. Left unchecked, it opens the door to other decay-causing organisms, so consider it an early warning sign. Because of its ability to stain, mildew is best removed by washing the log surface with a bleach solution. Chlorine bleaches have been shown to break down wood fibers, so try an oxygen bleach mixed in water at about a 1:10 ratio. TSP, or trisodium phosphate, also works well. It is usually mixed at four to six tablespoons per gallon of water. Douglas Mampe, author of *Wood Decay in Structures and Its Control*, suggests removing mildew by scrubbing it with a soft brush dipped in a solution of three ounces of TSP, one ounce of household detergent, one quart of household bleach, and three quarts of warm water. As with any cleaner, wear rubber gloves and glasses while handling these materials. To prevent its reoccurrence, add a fungicide or mildewcide to the stain coating.

Sapstain

Also known as *blue-stain*. This fungus is typically present in the logs when they are harvested and milled. The stains are normally surface stains, but they can infect wood fibers deep into the sapwood. Because of the many different hues of red, brown, blue, and black, some lumberyards consider sapstain attractive and charge a premium for it. Although sapstain does not cause any structural damage, it can increase the absorptive power of the wood, so the wood should be coated and completely sealed with a water repellent. Inspect these areas on a regular basis to make sure the application of water repellent is doing its job, otherwise, decay fungi have an easy place to attack the wood.

Brown Rot

This is the principal cause of fungi decay in log homes. In its early stages, it forms white spots on the wood surface, which is sometimes hard to distinguish. As it advances, it is characterized by a brown color, and the rotted wood becomes cracked, crumbly, and eventually powdery. This fungus can spread and damage wood rapidly, especially in moist or wet wood. One form of brown rot that deserves mention is heart rot. Heart rot infects the heartwood of live trees. If not totally removed during the manufacturing process, the spores can remain dormant until the log's moisture content reaches the fiber saturation point. At that point and until this form is detected, the fungus will spread to adjoining logs. Detection is usually in the form of a surface fungus attacking the same log.

Dry Rot

Dry rot is similar to brown rot in that it is a persistent, rapidly deploying decay fungus. The main difference is this fungus can infect dry wood, hence its name. But, like brown rot, it needs moisture to propagate and grow. In its decaying form, its appearance is much like a cracked windshield. The surface may feel solid, leading you to believe it is shallow, but underneath it can be heavily decayed. Look for cobweb or star-shaped powdery growths nearby. These are the source of moisture. Inspect this area and prepare to perform repairs here also. Caught in the early stages, this type of decay is best treated with the borate preservatives and liquid epoxy repair.

White Rot

This type of fungus gives a bleached appearance to the affected wood and is more prevalent in hardwoods, but certain strains have been found in softwoods. The wood is usually soft and spongy. Less pervasive than brown and dry rots, it can be hard to identify. If you suspect white rot, simply probe the area for the soft, spongy texture that breaks away easily in long strands. Underneath you will find white, stringy, weblike structures.

Don't confuse these with dried pitch pockets, which are similar but don't form the weblike structures.

Pocket Rot

Also known as white speck rot, this type of decay fungus infects live trees and is normally culled out during milling. Residual signs of this fungus are white specks on the surface of the wood. Even though this type of rot cannot survive in harvested logs, treat these areas with a good dose of borate preservatives because like any fungus, the specks can provide access to moisture seeping into the log component.

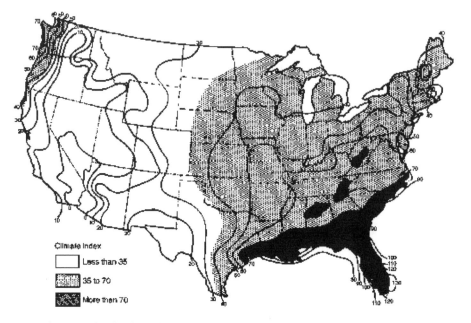

Figure 5–2. Climate index for decay hazard. Higher numbers indicate greater decay hazard.
Reprinted: *The Wood Handbook: Wood as an Engineering Material,* U.S. Dept. of Agriculture, Forest Service, Forest Products Laboratory, FPL-GTR-113

Soft Rot

This form is typically shallow in nature and found on heavily weathered logs. The wood beneath this fungus is usually firm but darker in color than the natural bleached look of unweathered wood.

The first step is to inspect the entire structure (see Chapter 2). Look for and mark all signs of external rot. Most of the time there will be one or two spots to work with, so marking is unimportant. However, if the number of spots is intimidating, mark them by stapling a three-by-five index card next to them, and call in the experts.

Next, decide which method to use to repair the damage—Epoxy wood fillers or log replacement. Epoxies can be less invasive, but be sure to treat the entire area of damage. Log replacement requires the removal of all the damage, and that can be labor intensive.

A rule of thumb I use is if the log surface is not sufficiently damaged and a majority of log material, either rotted or solid, is still in place, attempt epoxy remediation. If evidence of rot is deep and crumbly, use log replacement. There are exceptions to every rule, so use your best judgment and work with what you are comfortable with.

Insect Damage

Repairing insect damage is very similar to repairing rot and decay. First, know what insect has infested the structure. Then, determine the extent of the damage, repair it, and remove the attractant.

If you are a new owner of a log home, it is important to understand that fungal decay is a more common problem with log structures than is insect damage. However, most wood-destroying insects are attracted to wood by the same mechanisms of moisture, temperature, and a food source. In fact, most wood boring insects are attracted to wood only *after* fungal decay has set in. If any one of these three conditions is controlled, the problem is eliminated.

Extensive damage from insects usually occurs over a long period—not days or weeks but months and years. As a result, improperly maintained homes built ten, twenty, even thirty years ago are the most

Figure 5–3. Types of insect damage most likely to occur in a building. Upper left–Termite attack; feeding galleries (often parallel to the grain) contain excrement and soil. Upper right–Powder-post beetle attack; exit holes usually filled with wood flour and not associated with discolored wood. Lower left–Carpenter ant attack; nesting galleries usually cut across grain and are free of residue. Lower right–Beetle attack; feeding galleries (made in the wood while green) free of residue and surrounding wood darkly stained.
Reprinted: *The Wood Handbook: Wood as an Engineering Material,* U.S. Dept. of Agriculture, Forest Service, Forest Products Laboratory, FPL- GTR-113

susceptible. In fact, experiencing problems is one of the main reasons log homes are sold. Implementing an ongoing, regular, recorded maintenance program in new or recent construction is the best defense to any problem. See Figure 5–3 for the types of insect damage most likely to occur in a building.

The chart of wood-boring insects in Figure 5–4 is not a complete list but a reference to the most common wood-boring insects. The objective here is simply to point out the type of insect doing the damage and thereby determine what has to be done to take care of the problem. Once you have identified the most likely culprit, you have a starting point for your research. The research should focus on the amount of typical damage and the appropriate action to take. A good home owner's reference for all types of household pests is *Common-Sense Pest Control,* by William Olkowski, et al.

Usually, the first sign of an insect problem is finding a pile of sawdust and frass on the floor, a beam, or on the face of the logs. Finding sawdust and frass is not necessarily a sign to call the exterminator, tent the home, and fumigate. This is expensive, and most of the time unnecessary. Rather, it is a sign to pay attention, do research, and investigate. Scoop up this pile and save it in a resealable plastic bag. Find the bug hole it came from and capture a specimen if you can. Look at the condition of the wood surrounding the hole. Is it wet? Dry? Are there unsealed checks in the log? What is the condition of the reverse face of the log? What seems to have attracted the insect? A source of moisture? Food? If the hole is on the inside of the structure, is it near a window or door?

Now, get out a note pad and take some notes. It is best to write this information down so you don't forget anything. Items to note are:

1. date you found these signs
2. size and shape of the bug hole
3. location of the hole
4. evidence of and size, shape, location of other holes
5. log condition around area of hole or holes
6. description and/or a drawing of the specimen

The majority of problems experienced in new construction come from non-reinfesting insects. Non-reinfesting insects invade live trees for their food source and shelter for their eggs. Once the tree dies and dries out, it no longer provides a food source, so the insects move on and infect another tree. When a sufficient number of trees have been infected and die, the stand of trees are usually targeted for harvesting. When these trees are harvested, some of them may still have unhatched eggs or larvae. If the resulting logs are untreated and placed in a log home package, signs of an infestation don't appear until the adult in-

BEETLES

Group	Appearance	Detection	Habitat	Notes
Deathwatch family : *Anobiidae*	*1/16–3/8″ long *reddish brown to black	*round exit holes 1/16–1/8″ *frass—fine, oval loosely packed	*seasoned hardwoods and softwoods	*life cycle—1 to 3 years *damage—larval *medium risk reinfestation
Powderpost, false family : *Bostrichidae*	*1/8–1/4″ long *brown to black	*round exit holes 1/8–3/8″ *frass—fine, tightly packed galleries	*freshly seasoned hardwoods rarely in softwoods	*life cycle—1 year *damage—larval *no risk reinfestation
Flathead/ Metallic Wood family : *Buprestidae*	*1/4–1 1/4″ long *various colors metallic tint	*oval exit holes 1/8–1/2″ *frass—coarse in galleries	*live hardwood and softwood	*life cycle—1 to 30 yrs. *damage–larval *no risk reinfestation
Roundhead/ Longhorn family : *Cerambycidae*	*1/4–2″ long *brownish black *long antennae	*oval exit holes 1/8–1/2″ *frass—powdery fibrous	*sapwood of hardwood and softwood	*life cycle—1 to 30 yrs. *damage—larval *no risk reinfestation
Old house borer family : *Cerambycidae*	*5/8–1″ long *brownish black	*oval exit holes 1/4″ *frass—powdery formed in pellets	*primarily seasoned softwoods	*life cycle—3 to 10 yrs. *damage—larval/adult *high risk reinfestation
Powderpost, true family : *Lyctidae*	*1/8–1/4″ long *reddish brown to black	*round exit holes 1/32–1/8″ *frass—powdery talc like	*seasoned hardwood high starch count	*life cycle—1 year *damage—larval/adult *high risk reinfestation

ANTS

Group	Appearance	Detection	Habitat	Notes
Carpenter Ants	1/2–3/4″ long *black	*pronounced waist, galleries with grubs, tan egg cocoons *dark/square frass	*damp, decayed softwood	*galleries used for nesting, high *high risk reinfestation

BEES

Group	Appearance	Detection	Habitat	Notes
Carpenter Bees	*1″ long *black	*1/2″ round holes, woodpecker damage feeding on bees	*soffit/fascia material, log *checks and cracks	*swarming—summer *prefer non-coated softwoods
Wood wasps horntails	*1″> long *black or metallic blue	*1/4″ round exit holes *elongated spine at base of abdomen	*unseasoned softwoods	*life cycle—2 to 5 yrs. *damage—larval/adult *no risk reinfestation
Yellowjackets paper wasps	*1″ long *black/yellow or black	*swarming early spring *paper like nests in eaves	*nests in dark protected areas, eaves, attics	*some may be aggressive *life cycle—1 yr.
Sawfly	*1″ long *brown to black	*adults emerge May/June *similar appearance to horntails	*foliage feeders *unseasoned wood only	*life cycle—<1 year *no risk reinfestation

TERMITES

Group	Appearance	Detection	Habitat	Notes
Subterranean	*1/4–1/2″ long *brown to black	*earthen tubes on foundation exterior *wing piles beneath windows/doors, spring & fall	*most likely to infest damp woods near ground level	*responsible for the most damage *queen life cycle—3 to 10 years *colonize up to 200,000 *damage—adult
Drywood	*1/2″ long *tan to brown	*frass—oval shape, coarse *secretion-plugged entrance holes	*South/coastal U.S. *firewood piles *rotted stumps	*Does not need moisture *Hard to detect *enters wood through cracks
Dampwood	*1″ long *red/brown heads	*Large oval shaped frass	*Damp, decayed wood *South/coastal U.S.	*can spread to dry wood *swarming in summer/fall
Powderpost	*1/2″ long	*brown or black heads *digested wood powdery	*dry wood *South/coastal U.S.	
Formosan	*1/2″ long *yellowish	*same as subterranean	*South/coastal U.S. *typically nest above ground	*very aggressive, destructive *can colonize millions

Figure 5–4. Wood-boring insect identification. (termites, ants, beetles)

sects emerge. Then, all the non-reinfesters are doing is escaping to find a suitable food source. Depending on the moisture content of the log component, this phenomenon can last for two to five years. For this reason, it is important to capture a specimen. Preserve the specimen in a mixture of water and alcohol and bring it to the local county extension service. It is the best resource for identification and may have suitable literature to increase your knowledge. Because county extension services are usually attached to state universities, you might also be aiding the university's research programs. The non-reinfesting insect problem does not rest solely with manufacturers using standing dead timber. Any log material can potentially have some form of infestation.

The secret to eliminating an insect problem from the start is to use dry wood (15 percent moisture content or less) and treat the logs with a preservative, preferably a borate preservative.

In older structures, a thorough inspection is necessary. Look for fresh signs of bug holes, sawdust, and moisture. (See the section on "Existing Homes" in Chapter 2 for a more detailed list of things to look for.)

The next step is to determine the extent of damage. With the handle end of a scratch awl or screwdriver, tap on the wood surrounding the bug hole. Listen for signs of decayed, hollow wood and insect movement. If insect movement is suspected, magnify the sounds using a cup turned upside down. Even better, use a stethoscope. Repeat this process as you move away from the hole. Try to get an idea of the size of the area. In new construction, this area is usually small and only requires plugging the hole. As an extra measure, inject the hole and any surrounding log checks with a borate preservative, using a syringe or a plastic bottle with a long, tapered neck. If the damage is more extensive, follow the instructions on log repairs in Chapter 6 to determine your course of action.

Termites

Older structures are more prone to attacks by reinfesting wood-boring insects such as termites, carpenter ants, bees, and old house boring beetles. Applying a chemical barrier between the nest and the foundation usually gets rid of termites. This barrier, called termiticides, is injected into the ground around the perimeter of the house and piers for posts. To ensure the proper application, this is best left to professional exterminators. Once eradicated, the damage left behind, if it does not impair the structural integrity of the building, can usually be repaired with epoxies.

As a general rule, if the damaged area is small and shallow, use epoxy repairs. If it is large and deep, use log replacement. If the damage covers a substantial area, you are best served by calling in a professional with the right tools.

Because most termite species need to be in constant contact with some form of moisture for their survival, they can be difficult to detect. One obvious sign of termites is swarming. Swarming occurs when a number of young adults leave the existing nest in search of a new site. This occurs in the spring and fall, usually in the early evening after a rainstorm or shower. Another sign, and probably the most indicative of termites, are the earthen tubes found on foundation walls leading up to the logs. These earthen tubes are normally found on the shaded side of an infected home or under a porch or deck. Destroying these tubes takes away the termite's escape route. From there, look at the surrounding landscape. Are there any obvious signs of termite colonies? Rotted stumps, woodpiles? Don't discount an underground nest. Uncovering the source of the infestation is only the first step. As stated before, the perimeter of the structure will need to be treated with a termiticide. Once this is done you can survey the damage to the structure and decide on the remedial steps.

Sometimes a carpenter ant is mistaken for a termite. It happens enough to be considered commonplace. Figure 5–5 shows the differences.

Termites	Carpenter ants
2 pairs of wings - both sets are approximately the same size	2 pairs of wings - front set are larger than the hind set
antenna are straight	antenna are bent or "elbowed"
waist is broader between thorax and abdomen	waist is pinched between thorax and abdomen
body colors more varied - from cream to reddish brown	typically reddish brown to black

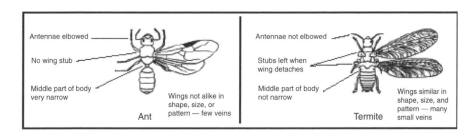

Figure 5–5. Comparison of termites and carpenter ants.

Carpenter Ants

Carpenter ants are also attracted to a damp wood environment. While the damage done usually requires the same remediation as for rot and decay, the insects themselves can be easier to control than termites. Carpenter ants do not use wood as a food source. Instead, they tunnel into wood for shelter and nesting. A nest found in the home is usually a satellite nest. This nest was most likely formed when the parent nest became too large to support the colony. The parent nest is typically found outside in a rotting stump, woodpile, or infected tree. Because ants from the satellite nest will travel back to the parent nest, don't destroy the first one you find. Watch where the ants travel. By following them, usually in the evening, you will most likely uncover the parent nest. Once the parent nest has been destroyed, a jelly bait near the satellite nest will coax the rest of the ants out where they can be disposed of. Injecting liquid borate type preservatives into the exit holes also works well on eradicating this insect. Depending on the amount of damage, expose the gallery and spray or inject the area directly. Left alone and undetected, carpenter ants usually take several years and a number of colonies to produce substantial damage. If this is the case, you may need to replace the logs.

Carpenter Bees

Carpenter bees tend to be attracted to places where there are voids such as cracks, crevices, and checks in the wood. They burrow from there and are more of a menace than a serious problem. Like any annoyance though, if left untreated, they can become a serious problem. Carpenter bees are not considered harmful because they do not sting. However, they do swarm and they attract woodpeckers. Once eradicated, seal the entrance hole or crack with liquid epoxy and/or epoxy wood filler or some other solid, nonwood substance. Carpenter bees will bore through wooden plugs. Typical entrances for these bees are up high on the structure, under the eaves, or in an attic space.

This category of insect also includes wood wasps, horntails, sawflies, and yellow jackets.

Beetles

Old house wood boring beetles are a subspecies of the roundheaded beetle. While the roundheaded beetle is a non-reinfesting insect, the old house beetle will reinfest. Borate preservatives work on this insect.

However, depending on the amount of time that has elapsed from their infestation to their detection, damage can be extensive. Although damp, decaying wood initially attracted them, beetles will also attack dry, unprotected wood. In this case, you should consult a professional exterminator.

The objective of this section was to outline the identification of the common species of insects that will infest log homes. However, there are also other species of insects that infest wood. The scope of damage done by this smaller group of wood-boring insects is similar to the more common species and the remediation, too, is the same.

Finish Failure

Not to be confused with the normal service life of applied finishes, there are two main causes for premature finish failure found in log homes:

1. excessive moisture
2. poor bonding of applied finish to log surface

"Normal service life" is the calculated amount of time a particular finish is expected to provide protection before reapplication is necessary. However, there are a number of factors that affect the performance of the finish and result in the "actual service life." These factors include:

1. appropriate choice of finish
2. application methods and conditions
3. exposure to weather

The choice of finish is usually dictated by what works in a particular area. Talk to other log home owners. What did they use? When did they apply it? How has the finish held up? See also the section on "Choosing an Exterior Wood Finish" in Chapter 3 for more tips.

Conditions that can result in finish failure include doing it in bad weather, improperly preparing log surfaces, the methods used to apply the finish, and not following the manufacturer's directions. Improper application techniques are usually the cause for poor bonding of the applied finish to log surfaces.

Over time, all finishes will deteriorate from exposure to UV radiation and dirt buildup from wind and rain. By regularly inspecting the integrity of the existing finish, you can determine the effectiveness of the finish.

Here are some of the more common signs of finish failure:

Mill Glaze

This condition is usually associated with procedures used during the manufacturing process. Peeling, cutting, planing, and kiln-drying operations may cause extractives to migrate to the surface of logs where they can dry to a hard, glazelike finish and become difficult to remove. As a result, applied finishes will not adhere properly to the log surfaces. Penetrating stains will not penetrate and film-forming stains will streak when brushed. Because mill glaze is considered a manufacturing issue, a larger area of log material can be affected, making surface preparation the key to resolving this problem. The reason for this situation is that initially the log surfaces were not properly prepared. Completely remove the existing finish and prepare the logs as you would for an initial application.

Discoloration

This condition is caused by extractive bleeding and/or sapstain and iron stain. Extractives are water soluble chemicals found in the heartwood of richly colored woods. In log homes, the common species include, but are not limited to, Western red cedar, redwood, Douglas fir, southern yellow pine, and Norway pine. Under high surface moisture conditions, the extractives will migrate toward and leach out onto the log surface. As the moisture evaporates, the extractives dry, leaving a reddish-brown stain. This condition is more pronounced on light-colored finishes. Although not a finish failure in the traditional sense, this condition is considered unsightly. As stated before, moisture is the primary culprit. Somehow, moisture found its way under the applied finish and into the heartwood. Extractive bleeding is usually a sign that the coating of applied finish was too thin.

Extractives can normally be removed if the occurrence was recent. Simply wash the surface with a mild detergent and rinse thoroughly. Allow the surface to dry completely before reapplying an additional coat. If the severity of extractive bleeding is extensive and hard to get rid of, the entire finish has to be removed. Apply a borate preservative before reapplying the finish coat.

Sapstain, or blue stain, is a fungal condition where the wood reveals a wide variation of blue-black stains. If the wood is kept dry, below 20 percent moisture content, this staining is not a problem. However, because it is a fungus, it can allow other decay fungi to infest the wood if the moisture content rises above 20 percent. Sapstain penetrates deep into the fibers of the sapwood and, therefore, cannot be removed. Limiting the ability of moisture to access the wood surface is the only remedy. Make sure that the coating of finish is adequate to provide protection.

Iron stains are a reaction of iron with wood tannins or extractives. They are most commonly seen when nails, screws, or other fasteners rust and leave a black stain around the fastener or running down the log surface. If possible, replace the fastener with a galvanized or other nonrusting fastener. A mixture of oxalic acid (one pound) and hot water (four gallons) will remove these stains. Also, some log brightener products have oxalic acid already formulated in them. Make sure to remove all signs of iron stain, as it will recur if not completely removed.

Moisture Blisters

Moisture blisters are caused by applying a film-forming or solid-coat finish before the log components have reached equilibrium moisture content. This is a major finish failure, with the only remedy being to remove the finish and allow the log components to reach EMC. Before reapplying a new finish coat, prepare the log components using the methods discussed in Chapter 3.

In some cases, I have seen moisture blisters form on the exterior opposite an interior high-humidity room, such as a bathroom, sauna, or Jacuzzi. The problem turned out to be an improperly applied sealant joint.

Moisture Cracks or Peeling

Moisture cracks usually occur when an inappropriate film-forming or solid-coat finish is applied. The finish does not expand and contract with the shrinking and swelling of the log components and develops stress fractures. These cracks allow moisture to seep in under the finish and sometimes cause peeling. Peeling is a sign that the log substrate was not properly prepared prior to applying the finish. In either case, depending on the severity of the failure, spot touch-ups or complete finish removal is called for. Peeling is also associated with improperly applying a new finish coat over an existing finish coat. The causes of this condition are either the finishes are not compatible, or the existing surface was not properly cleaned.

Mildew

Mildew is usually found in the areas of the structure that are more shaded and have some light moisture. The formation of mildew looks similar to dirt buildup, with dark specks on the log surface. If you are unsure whether it is dirt or mildew, apply a drop or two of household bleach to the stain. If the spot turns white in a minute or two, the stain is mildew. To stop the mildew from recurring, apply a cleaning solution with bleach. See Chapter 3 for log-cleaning tips.

Splash Back

Splash back is usually found on the log courses close to ground level. This condition is caused by water running off the roof, hitting the ground, and "splashing back" on the log surfaces. The dirt hitting the logs acts like sandpaper, making small holes in the finish. These holes allow moisture to get inside and cause cracking, peeling, and, in extreme cases, wood decay. Clean the dirt off the surface, sand down the entire area, and apply a preservative and multiple coats of finish. Secondary to this is the installation of gutters, downspouts, and some form of ground cover to prevent the dirt from "splashing back" on the log components.

Sealant Failure

As discussed in Chapter 3, there are two main causes of sealant failure: adhesive failure and cohesive failure.

Adhesive failures are evidenced by the sealant pulling away from the log substrate. The sealant did not adhere to the wood surface.

Cohesive failures are evidenced by the sealant pulling away from itself or tearing. Too much stress was exerted on the sealant material.

Although some of the following causes are more prevalent in one type of failure or the other, they all apply to both types of failure. In either case, a failed sealant has to be removed and reapplied.

Surface Preparation

Ideally log surfaces should be clean and bare for the application of sealants. However, when used in conjunction with a compatible finish,

(Above) Adhesion failure. Notice that the caulk has pulled away from the log. (Below) Cohesion failure. The caulk has torn because of too many stresses. When this particular house was inspected, the home owner stated he used a "Fifty-year warranty" caulk. It was put on five years ago. Remember, if the sealant is not specific for the job, it will most likely fail.

the application of the sealant can be administered *over* the finish, and a firm bond will be accomplished. Noncompatibility of sealant with finish is a condition usually associated with catastrophic adhesive failures. The sealant bead will pull away easily from the underlying bead or log substrate.

Material Chemistry

The sealant material you choose must be compatible with log home sealing. In this case, there are subcategories to consider: age, quality, and type.

Age

Sealant materials developed years ago had a substantially shorter service life, usually five years. After that time, the material would start to break down and present a "chalky" surface. Most of the time, the material loses its elasticity, becomes brittle, and breaks away from the log substrate. Also included in this category would be sealant materials applied after their useful shelf life. In addition to the adhesive failures, cohesive failures can be revealed when removing the affected bead. Instead of being removed in strips, the material will come off in chunks and break down into a powdery residue.

Quality

Quality issues of sealant failure are seen in materials that did not live up to their advertised claims. These materials are usually from a "no name" brand or off the excess inventory shelf. Adhesive and cohesive failures will occur. A good-quality log home sealant will have a long-term warranty period. Today that period is usually twenty-five or more years.

Type

In an effort to save a few bucks, a home owner may have purchased the wrong type of material because it was advertised as "bonding to wood." As discussed earlier, log dynamics are different and greater than the dynamics of other dimension wood products, like siding, for instance. Adhesive failures are the primary indicator of a wrong type of sealant used.

(Top) Even though proper design was kept in mind, this bead failed due to improper surface preparation and because the caulk was not formulated for log home use. (Bottom) Another view of the same bead.

Compatibility

The sealant was not "matched up" with the finish material prior to application. Compatibility has been and will continue to be, for the foreseeable future, a major cause of adhesive failures in log homes.

Improper Design

The bead was applied unevenly to shrink and swell with the log movement. The cohesive failure of a high-quality log home sealant is typically an indication that the sealant was applied too thinly. This is the only application where an "overcoating" can be considered. If you try this, make sure the existing bead is cleaned thoroughly so that the "overcoat" will bond to it.

Chapter 6

Log Component Repairs

Checks and Cracks

There are many factors affecting the soundness of logs, including knots, slope of grain, compression, tension, twist, pitch pockets, decay, shake, checks, and splits. Unsound characteristics should be culled out in the manufacturing process. However, checking and cracking are natural characteristics of dry or drying wood and, depending on their size, are not normally considered serious defects. Attempts are made to minimize their appearance, but because of the shrinking and swelling nature of logs, they cannot be stopped. Logs will constantly move in response to changes in moisture occurring from season to season, weather patterns, and home use.

As logs dry and acclimate to their surroundings, stresses are released, fibers shrink and separate, and checks are created. Our purpose here is not to develop a grading standard to choose which logs will check and which ones will not. Our purpose is to accept that they will check and determine how to handle this situation.

The important point to keep in mind is that checks and cracks are an open invitation to the other predators that cause damage to a log home—mold, fungi, decay, insects. As a result, remediation is accomplished by filling them.

Any check that can accept a bead of caulk should be filled. That generally means any check more than a quarter of an inch wide. For those checks less than a quarter of an inch and deemed needing to be filled, run a bead over the entire area to fill. Then, using a circular motion with your hand, press the bead into the entire area. When that is done, scrape off the excess and wipe down the area with a wet rag. Try to leave a thin film over the area just to be sure of good adhesion and coverage. For those checks greater than a quarter of an inch and able to accept a length of backer rod, pack the rod in first before running a bead of caulk. This will cut down on the use of caulking material and provide a better caulked joint. Remember to pack the backer rod deep enough so that the caulk bead attains two point adhesion and the depth is half the width of the bead, but no less than a quarter of an inch. (See the section on "Applying the Sealant" in Chapter 3.)

Maintenance on checks in excess of 1 inch wide is somewhat more involved. A check that wide may be an indication of other problems.

First, take a scratch awl or screwdriver and poke around inside the check. You are looking for signs of the depth of the check, moisture, and rot. Checks do not generally go deeper than the center of the log. They can, however, join with a check from the opposite side and effectively split the log in half. After this inspection, if you have not found other problems, clean all debris out of the check. I use a compressor set at 125 PSI. After cleaning out the debris, check the moisture level as deep into the check as possible. (See the section on "Testing for Moisture Content" in Chapter 1.) If the moisture content is in excess of 20 percent, tent the check by draping plastic over it and seal it so as not to allow any moisture to get in but still allow for airflow to dry it out. Next, prep the check by injecting a liquid epoxy along the entire length. I have found the two-part penetrating mixture (resin and hardener) for exterior use works best. On average, I use a two-pint blend for every 3 feet of a check that is 4 inches deep. Inject it onto the top and bottom inside faces of the check using a clean oil-mixing syringe. These are available at most auto parts stores. Allow the epoxy to soak into the wood but do not let it drip outside on to the face of the log. While waiting for it to cure, mix and knead a wood filler epoxy. Liquid epoxy suppliers usually carry the wood filler epoxy also. Following the instructions for the wood filler, pack the material tightly into the check leaving a half-inch-deep gap at the top. When done with that and before the filler has cured, mix and knead the next and final application of filler with some fine sawdust or a powdered color pigment. Pack this tightly also, leaving a "mound" to sand when the filler has cured. The sawdust is added for better acceptance of stain and "hiding" the work done. Before staining over the entire length of wood filler, test a small piece with a brush, rag, or sponge. If you are happy with the results, continue staining. If not, try running a thin bead of caulk and tooling it before staining.

Loose Wood Repair

For the purpose of this discussion, loose wood is defined as log material that has broken from the existing log and shows no sign of rot underneath. This can happen due to a number of factors either naturally or mechanically. This type of problem is not usually caused by a design flaw or manufacturing process. However, as with any problem requiring repair work, look at the reason for the problem and decide if any changes in the structure need to be made to prevent this problem from recurring. The important point here is that loose wood is like an open wound. Left untreated, weather and insects can start their work, and before you know it you have a bigger problem to deal with. I gauge the type of remediation by the size of the loose piece.

First of all, how loose is it? Can it be removed completely and easily? Without totally removing it, test to see how loose it is. Gently tug on the piece. Do not remove it if you do not have to. How and where is it still attached? What does the wood behind it look like? Is the piece big enough to accept being held by screws? If you leave it in place, will it be susceptible to future damage or decay? Remember, the objective is to protect the structure against sunlight, moisture, and insects.

If the piece is small enough where a wood filler epoxy patch will restore the surface profile, remove the loose piece. Before grabbing the loose piece and tugging on it, cut through the area where the wood is still attached so that you get a clean break. If the resulting hole is shallow enough, drill a series of $1/4$-inch by $3/8$-inch diameter holes about 2 inches apart. Because we are dealing with solid wood, the holes should be about half an inch deep. Now, clean the cavity of all debris and sawdust. Use some form of dry method—a brush, rag, vacuum cleaner or air compressor. Next, prep the cavity by injecting a liquid epoxy along the entire length. As described above, the two-part mixture of resin and hardener for exterior use works best. On average, I use a half-pint blend for a 1-inch by 3-foot cavity about half an inch thick. Inject the epoxy into the quarter-inch holes using a clean oil-mixing syringe. Allow the epoxy to soak into the wood but don't let it drip outside onto the face of the log. While waiting for it to cure, mix and knead a wood filler epoxy. Following the instructions for the wood filler, pack the material tightly into the cavity. If this is the first time you have worked with a wood filler epoxy, mix and knead a small portion. Get used to working with it before mixing a larger portion. Pay attention to the "pot life," the amount of time to work the material before it starts to cure and harden. If it is important to hide the patch, leave some room to apply a second coating of the wood filler epoxy. When done with that and before the filler has cured, mix and knead the next and final application of filler with some fine sawdust or a powder color pigment. Pack this tightly also, leaving a mound to sand when the filler has cured. Dabbing on the stain with a rag or sponge does a good job of hiding the patch.

Some loose wood repairs are deep and the wood is best left as is. In this case, pry the loose piece out as far as you can without fracturing it anymore. Stick a shim in to hold the piece in place while you clean behind it. A compressor works best to clean out the dirt and debris. When done, remove the shim and allow the piece to settle back in its original position. Set and countersink a couple of galvanized or stainless steel screws to hold the loose piece to solid wood. Along the top, side, and bottom of the loose piece, following the crack of the loose piece, drill a series of $1/4$-inch by $3/8$-inch holes about 2 inches apart and at least the depth of the loose piece. For the best bond, drill about a half an inch into the solid wood behind the loose piece. Try to follow the slope of the loose piece as you drill. Inject liquid epoxy in these holes. Follow the directions above for injection instructions. Reinject the holes at twenty to thirty-minute intervals until they will accept no more epoxy. Try not to let the epoxy bleed out onto the face of the log. Wipe the surface with a clean, dry rag immediately if it does. You do not want to use any solvent to clean the face of the log. Let this cure overnight. On the following day, check to see if all the holes are still filled with epoxy. If not, repeat the process until they are. Once they are all filled and the epoxy has cured, sand the entire surface—60–80 grit paper works best. The goal is to return the surface to the original profile and leave a rough enough surface to accept a stain coating.

In the event the loose wood is caused by underlying rot and decay, see the section on "Rot and Decay" in Chapter 5 for remedial action.

Exposed Log Ends

Exposed log ends include notched corner logs, roof purlins and rafters, porch beams, and posts. Exposed log ends are particularly susceptible to rot and decay problems because the primary channel for moisture absorption is exposed. In the case of notched corner logs, there are only two things to do to solve this problem—remove them or seal them. Whenever possible, I try to save them. Saving them is best done by injecting them with liquid epoxy coupled with the use of Impel Rods. In the event they are rotted beyond repair, it is best to remove all of them and face off the corner with vertical pieces to look like a log post. The time and expense involved in replacing corner log ends is not usually justified for aesthetic appeal. In the other cases, the log ends are exposed because they are serving some load-bearing function. This repair work is best left to the professionals. You can, however, seal them yourself. An inexpensive solution is to use some leftover caulk. Gun a bead on the log end and, with your hand moving in a circular motion, work the bead into the entire surface. Seal every crack, so spray water on the surface as you work it in. When done, wipe the surface with a wet rag but leave a thin film. Because logs expand and contract, be prepared to go over the log ends with a razor blade to remove the excess after it has cured a day or two.

It wouldn't hurt all the exposed log ends to receive one or more Impel Rod inserts (see page 120). Simply drill a hole in as inconspicuous a spot as possible, insert the rod, and plug the hole. Just be aware that the size of the hole depends on the size of the rod, and the size of the rod depends on the size of the timber.

Epoxy Repairs

The easiest epoxy repairs are those that do not require a lot of preparation. Because epoxies reconstitute existing rotted wood fibers, it is not normally necessary to remove all evidence of rot before injecting the area. The first step is to remove the loose, crumbly pieces. Try not to disturb the rest of the rotted material that is left. Next, find the extent of the rot. Take a scratch awl and poke through the center of the exposed rot. Measure how deep it is. Now, measure the depth at both ends of the rotted section. You should hit solid wood quickly. If not, then the rot has found a channel toward the center of the log and extends farther back under a solid wood surface shell.

Liquid Epoxy

In this case, you will need a drill and a quarter-inch drill bit. The length depends on how deep you guess the rot will go. Start with a standard (less expensive) 4-inch bit. Drill slowly through the surface shell and watch the wood particles as they come off the bit. Notice a change from solid wood to decay back to solid wood as you drill deeper. Make a note of the depth when you reach solid wood again. Repeat this process along the length of the affected log until you can drill a hole without hitting any decay. Don't worry about the holes; you will deal with them later. Now, go back to the center, where you started poking with the scratch awl, move up or down a couple of inches, offset the drilling pattern, and start the process again. The objective is to find the outline of the decayed area.

Once you have done this, spray or brush a log preservative on the affected area. Because rot is a serious problem, apply the preservative several times to ensure deep penetration. The borate preservatives work well to combat decay-causing fungi.

Now prepare your liquid epoxy mix. Again, use a two-part system (resin and hardener). The epoxy material should have a pot life of an hour or so. The reason for this is the longer the pot life, the deeper the penetration before the material cures and hardens. The more porous and decayed material will accept more epoxy than will solid wood, so inject those areas first. Do not let the epoxy set up on the face of the good log material. Wipe off any runs immediately with a clean rag.

When done with the rags, lay them out outdoors. Do not put them in the garbage or pile them in the corner someplace. Until they harden, most epoxies are combustible if they generate enough heat. Plan on using a new mixing container, mixing stick, and two syringes for each day of this project. Or, you can use a solvent to thoroughly clean the tools at the end of each day or when you take a break.

Once all the holes have been injected, wait thirty to sixty minutes and repeat the process. Do this until all the holes are filled with liquid epoxy. When the material has hardened, the holes will be sealed.

Next, at both ends of the formerly rotted section, drill a hole in un-treated solid wood and insert an Impel Rod. The size of rod used depends on the size of the log material. These holes should be 3 to 6 inches away from the epoxy-treated wood. The Impel Rod is a borate product that when wet will diffuse throughout the wood and kill any fungal spores that may remain. The reason for doing this is because the hardened epoxy will shed water to adjoining wood surfaces, which may facilitate the recurrence of decay in those surfaces. The Impel Rod will stop this process. Following the instructions that come with the Impel Rod, plug the hole with a wood plug.

Now sand the surface to the profile of the log material. Do not use sandpaper with a grit greater than 80. You need a relatively rough surface to apply the finish coat. Before applying the finish coat, brush off any sawdust and caulk the plugs and any holes left by the epoxy.

Now you are ready to apply the finish coat. Most liquid epoxies will not take a stain well. Dab a little stain over a spot with epoxy. If you are satisfied with this finish, dab stain over the entire area. If not, use a coarser grit sandpaper and try again. You will not be able to "hide" this repair work. If that is important, you will need to do a log replacement.

Why don't I consider wood filler epoxy here? Most log homes are stained so that the underlying grain shows through. A wood filler epoxy has no grain to reveal, and the size of these types of repairs are generally unappealing for this kind of "patch." They stick out like a sore thumb even if done correctly. Don't get me wrong, it can be done and I have done it. But when looks are important, I don't like this approach.

Wood Filler Epoxy

Wood filler epoxies are a puttylike substance that, once cured, are harder than the log surface itself. Wood fillers are typically used in small areas and in areas close to the ground. I have found that I get the best results when the surface I am applying it to is first treated with the liquid epoxy. This should be done the same way the above repair is made. Drill a series of holes, inject the liquid epoxy, then prepare the wood filler epoxy. I have also found that the entire void should not be completely filled with wood filler in one application.

Use a two-part, exterior use, marine-quality wood filler. Paying attention to the pot life, mix the two parts (resin and hardener) following the manufacturer's instructions. Make sure to wear a pair of rubber gloves—the inexpensive applicator's variety works fine. Pack the void as the liquid epoxy is setting up to within a half-inch of the surface. Next, mix an additional amount to complete the void, but add a small amount of fine sawdust to the mix. This sawdust will accept the finish application and be a close match to the existing finish. Pack the void so that the final application leaves a mound that can be sanded down later.

I have also use dried color pigments. They work well, but you will need to practice combining pigments and amounts before using them. If you work with color pigments, make sure the mixture is a little lighter than the finish that will be applied.

Next, drill a hole approximately 3 to 6 inches from both ends of the repair for inserting Impel Rods. For the same reason as a liquid epoxy repair, the wood filler is impervious to moisture and will, therefore, shed that moisture to the surrounding wood. This will stop the decay process from infecting that area. Following the manufacturer's instructions, plug the holes. If there is any wood filler/sawdust mix left, use it here to plug the holes.

The final step is sanding the cured wood filler to the profile of the log surface. Do not use a sandpaper grit greater than 80. A rougher surface will accept the finish better and hide your work.

Log Replacement Repairs

Log replacement is impressive, labor intensive, more satisfying, and sometimes unnecessary. When should log replacement be considered?

First of all, there are two types of log replacement—partial log and full log. With proper instructions, most home owners can perform a reliable partial log replacement. Full log replacements are best left to the professionals. The primary reason for log replacement is aesthetics. Holes drilled for liquid epoxy and wood filler epoxy patches are sometimes considered unsightly. When the job is done, and done right, the uninitiated won't know there was a rotted log.

As in a liquid epoxy repair, first determine the extent of the damage. Because this repair is replacing wood, start by removing all the loose pieces of decay. Depending on the length of available

(Above) This has been deteriorating for several years. The damage was deep enough for log siding replacement. (Below) This surface is ready for the log siding.

replacement pieces, center the decayed area in that length or measure from the closest butt joint. The objective in the finished appearance is an inconspicuous repair.

Mark both ends of the log component to be replaced. With the tip of a chain saw, plunge a vertical cut about the depth of the radius of the log component one-quarter inch inside the marks. The objective is to remove the entire face of the affected log, so the vertical cuts should be from the course above to the course below. The ideal chain saw is small and packed with power for high rpm's. Depending on the particular job, I use either a Husqvarna 335xpt or 346xp. Starting with the bottom of the bar (never the tip), resting on the upper curvature of the log, plunge a cut into the log until the tip can be rotated in just under the course above. Once completed, move the saw down at three-quarters throttle until the course below is contacted. Break the seal on the caulk between the courses and peel the wood away. You may need a hammer and chisel to square the inside corners of the rotted section. To ease the process of removing the face of the affected log, make a series of vertical cuts between the end marks. (*Note:* While doing this, watch out for the spikes, screws, or whatever else was used to join the logs. There are construction-type metal detectors available, but they can be pricey. Most joining hardware is in the center of the log, so odds are they will not be hit during this initial step.) By exposing the material under the surface, this step also exposes the extent of damage and any additional depth that needs to be removed.

While removing material, try to maintain a vertical or plumb line on the backside of the remaining material. This will aid in the rest of the project. Now that the face of the log has been removed, look at the area of decay. Does the decay extend to the edges of the material that was removed? If so, probe with the scratch awl to find the depth and additional length that needs to be removed. If the probing reveals an extensive amount of rot, repeat the process of measuring based on the available replacement material. Make the vertical cuts and chisel away the material. If you find an extensive amount of rot and decay, *stop.* Evaluate whether to continue or call a professional.

If, after the initial slab is removed and the probing reveals a small amount of additional decay around the edges less than half an inch, continue with the log replacement. Those areas can be injected with the liquid epoxy. Don't inject these areas yet, just know that it can be done. Now probe the exposed face to find out if the rot and decay extends through the entire width of the log. Most of the time it won't.

Around the area of decay drill a series of holes as was described above for liquid epoxy repairs. Don't worry about the rest of the exposed log at this time. Using a quarter-inch drill bit, drill slowly through the rotted area and watch the particles coming off the drill bit. While drilling, notice the difference between rotted wood and solid wood. Once you reach solid wood behind the decay, continue drilling another quarter- to half-inch. When you have reached the end of the decayed section, go back to the center, offset the pattern, and repeat the process until you have drilled a series of holes covering the entire decayed area.

The next step is to apply the preservative. Several applications of a borate-based preservative are normally adequate for deep penetration and killing the invading fungi.

Next, inject these holes with the liquid epoxy. While waiting for the current series of injections to set up, brush a coat of epoxy on the newly exposed log surface. Continue this process until the holes are completely full of epoxy.

Cover the entire surface with plastic and allow the epoxy to fully cure. Don't allow any moisture to get in, but do allow for airflow. This is best done by wrapping plastic around a one by or two by four piece of lumber. Extend the plastic about 3 feet past both ends and nail the plastic-wrapped lumber to the face of the log above and below. At the ends of the plastic, stick a short piece of lumber out perpendicular to the log being worked on. This should provide enough protection until the next step.

After the liquid epoxy has cured, take measurements of the void left by the log removal. These measurements include: (1) length minus one-quarter inch, (2) height on both ends and middle, and (3) depth on both ends and middle. Next, move on to the replacement material and mark off these measurements. When you are satisfied that these measurements are correct, snap a chalk line to join the measurements. Before making any cuts, look over the piece and try to visualize it fitting into the space. If it looks right, make the cuts. With a chain saw, at the local sawmill, or if you have the proper tools, undercut the lines by at least one-quarter inch. In other words, oversize the replacement material so that it can be worked down to the proper final size.

Take the resulting slab and test fit it. While it is over the space, rock it back and forth, up and down. Start feeling for where additional material needs to be removed. Look at the face of the replacement material. Check to make sure it is lining up with the adjoining faces. Also, make sure there will be no exposed, flat surfaces on the top where moisture can accumulate in the final fit. When placing the replacement log for the final fit, the replacement should be recessed about an eight- to a quarter-inch back from the existing face.

When that is done, set the replacement log aside and spray it with a preservative. I use a water-based borate product. Next, trowel a quarter-inch thick caulk bead over the entire surface of the exposed wood, including the log ends. Take the replacement piece and place it in the space. Tap gently along the entire length then remove it. Turn it over and look where the caulk made contact. Most important in this inspection is caulk along the entire top and bottom sides and log ends. Wherever the caulk did not make contact, squeeze an additional amount on. Place the piece back in the space. With a scrap piece of blocking, pound the replacement log into place. Step back and look at the replacement log. Does it look right? Now, anchor the piece with screws. Use galvanized or stainless steel screws. If the log removal was 2 inches deep, use 4-inch screws. Anchor the replacement in the four corners and approximately every 2 feet along the top and bottom. Set the corners on one end first. Don't countersink the screws yet. Go to the other end and test it to see if it has moved out. If it has, set one screw in one of the corners. Then start setting screws along the top and bottom. When all the screws are set and the placement looks right, countersink all of the screws. I have found that while finish screws leave a smaller countersink hole, they do not grab enough wood to firmly anchor a replacement log. Also, try to get the screws as close to the edge of the wood as possible. When this is done, seal around the entire perimeter of the replacement log. If the screws are placed correctly, they will be covered by the sealant bead.

Here are some tips to make the job easier: When injecting or replacing log material around windows and doors, check the integrity of the units to make sure the cause of the decay has not spread to them. Most units are set with some form of "bucking" material. This is usually two-by-four lumber. If there is any moisture or decay on it, replace it. Improper sealing around the trim is the main reason for this problem. Another reason could be improper drainage off the log at the base of the unit, especially if the log was notched to accept the unit. There should be about a five-degree slope from the unit to the outside of the log. If a window or door has to be removed for log repair, drill a hole and insert Impel Rods in the bottom logs on both sides and in the middle before replacing the unit.

If the window trim sits on the face of the log, cut a bevel along the top edge of the trim to facilitate runoff.

Evaluating Contractors

So, you've decided to hire a contractor to perform the necessary work, and you don't want to be taken advantage of. What and who should you look for? After all, a good contractor in this business should have a strong, sound basis in several fields—forestry, entomology, chemistry, rough carpentry, finish carpentry, and painting, to name but a few.

Not to disparage well-intentioned contractors, but there are many contractors who approach this type of work with the attitude of "how difficult can this be?" Unfortunately, or fortunately, log home restoration and repair work is a specialized craft requiring specialized knowledge and specialized tools. The following checklist should be a part of your general requirements. Add to this list any items you consider to be important additions specific to your job or site.

Before contacting anyone, have a specific list of the work to be done (and not done), priorities, and (hopefully) a budget.

Basic Requirements

Name, address, phone. In addition, is the contractor *self-employed, or incorporated*? *Type of insurance coverage.* Liability? Workmen's Compensation? *Type of licenses.* Driving? Contractor? State Department of Revenue?

Other Requirements

Time in business. How long has the contractor been doing the type of work you require? *Specialty.* What type of work does the contractor specialize in? Does your work fit that specialty? What tools (general and specialized) will the contractor use for your work? *Referrals.* The ideal referral list includes not just satisfied customers, but dissatisfied customers, too. *Pictures.* Are there before and after pictures of jobs performed? *Representation.* Does the contractor represent a particular manufacturer or supplier? Will the contractor use your materials and/or supplies? *Crew experience.* What is the level of experience of different crew members?

Estimates

Extent of work. What does the contractor need to determine the scope of the work? Your description? Pictures? Site visit? *Bidding.* How will the contractor price the work? Time and material? Firm bid? Will the contractor break down the individual components of the bid? How long is the bid good for? *Timing.* If selected, when would the contractor be available to perform your work? How much time is anticipated to do this work? *Change orders.* How does the contractor handle changes in work description? Authorization for changes? Timing of changes, when and how long? Materials needed? How will changes be billed?

Answers to your questions in these areas will help you decide if the contractor is qualified to perform your work. Additionally, you will be able to decide if you can establish a working relationship with that particular contractor. Did the contractor respond promptly and professionally to your questions?

Once you have decided on a particular contractor, the next list of issues that need to be answered include the following:

Your Conditions

Timing. Can the contractor start the work on the prescribed date? How long will the job take? *Job site.* How often will the site be cleaned up? Who will dispose of waste material? *Accommodations.* Who is responsible for over-night accommodations? Meals? *Communication.* How do you expect to be communicated with regarding progression of the job and changes? Inspection results? Returned phone calls?

The Contractor's Conditions

Invoicing. How often will invoices be presented? When is payment due? *Warranties, guarantees.* Are work and materials under warranty? Guaranteed? What is the nature of those pledges? *Callbacks.* What qualifies as a callback item? If necessary, when will the work be performed? Who will be responsible for the resulting bill?

Contract Agreement

Finally, get it in writing. It is not uncommon to misinterpret someone else's verbal statements. The agreement does not have to be drawn up by a lawyer. A letter stating your understanding and/or position is sufficient. By documenting your position you do not have to remember what was said, when it was said, or what you thought was said. Documentation is for everyone's peace of mind.

The purpose of this exercise is not to set up a structure whereby everyone needs to constantly look over his or her shoulder and become mistrustful. Rather, it is to establish a common ground and an honest working relationship.

Finish/Sealant Estimating Chart

FINISH / SEALANT ESTIMATING

Log Size _____   Perimeter _____

		L		**H / W**		**T**	**C**
1.	Walls						
	a	_____	x	_____	=	_____	_____
	b	_____	x	_____	=	_____	_____
	c	_____	x	_____	=	_____	_____
	d	_____	x	_____	=	_____	_____
	e	_____	x	_____	=	_____	_____
	f	_____	x	_____	=	_____	_____
	g	_____	x	_____	=	_____	_____
2.	Gables						
	a	_____	x	_____	/ 2 =	_____	_____
	b	_____	x	_____	/ 2 =	_____	_____
	c	_____	x	_____	/ 2 =	_____	_____
3.	Roofline (total)	_____	x	_____	=	_____	
4.	Porch (total)	_____	x	_____	x 2 =	_____	
5.	Deck (total)	_____	x	_____	=	_____	
6.	Posts (total)	_____			=	_____	
7.	Railing (total)	_____	x	_____		_____	

Total Square Footage (**L x H / W**) [_____]

Total Lineal Footage (**L x C**) [_____]

L = Length   **H / W** = Height / Width   **T** = Total   **C** = Courses

Cleaner	_____ sq.ft.	_____ cvr.rate	_____ quantity
Preservative	_____ sq.ft.	_____ cvr.rate	_____ quantity
Finish	_____ sq.ft.	_____ cvr.rate	_____ quantity
Sealant	_____ l.ft.	_____ cvr.rate	_____ quantity
Sealant	_____ l.ft.	_____ cvr.rate	_____ quantity
Backer Rod	_____ l.ft.		

Caulk Coverage Rate

Lineal feet per full gallon (231 cu. in.)		Width of Joint						
		1/4″	3/8″	1/2″	5/8″	3/4″	7/8″	1″
Depth of	1/4″	308	205	154	123	102	88	77
Joint	3/8″		136	102	82	68	58	51
	1/2″			77	61	51	44	39

Courtesy: *Sashco Sealants*, LBR005

Chink Coverage Rate

Lineal feet per full gallon (231 cu. in.)		Width of Joint							
		1/2″	1″	1 1/2″	2″	2 1/2″	3″	3 1/2″	4″
Depth of	1/4″	154	77	51	39	31	25	22	19
Joint	3/8″	102	51	34	25	20	17	14	13
	1/2″	77	39	25	19	15	13	11	9

Courtesy: *Sashco Sealants*, LC005

32 ounces = 1 quart   128 ounces = 1 gallon

10 quart tubes/case   10—10 oz. tubes/case

Cleaners - quantity determined by material used per sq. ft. of wall space

Preservatives - quantity determined by material used per sq. ft. of wall space

Finish - most finishes use these average coverage rates: (verify with supplier before ordering)

200–300 sq. ft. - smooth surfaces

150–200 sq. ft. - rough or handcrafted surfaces

Finish/Sealant estimating steps

1. *Measure and note log size and perimeter.*
2. *Measure and note wall lengths, heights and number of log courses.*
3. *Transpose wall length, estimate height of gables and number of log courses.*
4. *Insert perimeter measurement for length, measure overhang for width.*
5. *Measure length and width of all porch floor space.*
6. *Measure length and width of all deck floor space.*
7. *Add total lineal footage of all post material.*
8. *Measure total length of railing material, include average height for all material.*
   *Do not subtract for openings on wall log measurements.
   **Subtract percentage of gable for gable openings exceeding 50% of gable, only.
   The / 2 = column applies regardless of opening allowance.
***Sq. ft. values apply to finishes of the same color only.

FINISH / SEALANT ESTIMATING

		Log Size	10"		Perimeter		112"	

		L		H/W		T	C
1.	Walls						
	a	24	x	8	=	192	10
	b	32	x	8	=	256	10
	c	24	x	8	=	192	10
	d	32	x	8	=	256	10
	e		x		=		
	f		x		=		
	g		x		=		
2.	Gables						
	a	24	x	9	/ 2 =	108	11
	b	24	x	9	/ 2 =	108	11
	c		x		/ 2 =		
3.	Roofline (total)	112	x	2	=	224	
4.	Porch (total)	32	x	8	x 2 =	512	
5.	Deck (total)	32	x	10	=	320	
6.	Posts (total)	72			=	72	
7.	Railing (total)	84	x	3		252	

Total Square Footage (**L x H / W**)   2492

Total Lineal Footage   **(L x C)**   1384

L = Length   **H / W** = Height / Width   **T** = Total   **C** = Courses

Cleaner	2492	sq.ft.	200	cvr.rate	12 bags	quantity
Preservative	2492	sq.ft.	640	cvr.rate	4 gals.	quantity
Finish	2492	sq.ft.	150	cvr.rate	17 gals.	quantity
Sealant	1384	l.ft.	51	cvr.rate	25 gals.	quantity
Sealant	1384	l.ft.	154	cvr.rate	9 gals.	quantity
Backer Rod	1384	l.ft.				

Notes for sample finish/sealant estimate:

1. Method chosen for *cleaning* was media blasting. Coverage for 40 lb. bag estimated at 200 sq.ft.

2. *Penetreat* chosen as preservative. Purchased in powder form, this quantity is mixed with water to arrive at final quantity.

3. Quantity based on a rough profiled log and **one coat application**. Quantity overestimated allowing for touch-up staining.

4. Coverage rate based on a 1″ wide chink bead. Quantity underestimated because material will be used between log courses only. Anticipate a small overage for immediate touch-up work.

5. Method chosen was to chink between courses and caulk checks, cracks and around openings. This is an estimated number, hard to calculate before starting the job. Best option is to order a smaller quantity. Estimate total need based on actual usage. Ideally, you want no more than 2–3 tubes for touch-up work.

6. Figuring on the amount and type of backer rod to order is purely subjective. Decide what applications will need the material and estimate the footage.

* If pricing is an important issue, try to combine as many of these items in a single purchase to take advantage of applicable discounts.

Sample Product Record

Thank you for the opportunity to serve you. I hope you will be as happy with your log home as I had building and sealing it. I am supplying the following pages, brochures, and technical sheets to answer your future questions as they arise. As time passes, details are sometimes forgotten about materials used, how they were applied, and certain maintenance questions.

If you have any questions not answered in this material, please feel free to call me at _____.

LOG MATERIAL

Lodgepole Pine / Engelmann Spruce / Alpine Fir

Moisture content: 15% or less

Grading: Timber Product Inspectors, stamped grade 40

JOINING MATERIALS

12″ Blue Ox screws on 18″ centers, doubled in corners and at openings. Log Stacker Adhesive.

SEALING MATERIALS

Exterior: Penetreat preservative applied to point of refusal.

Capture stain (Chestnut) then applied with airless sprayer and back brushed.

Backer rod stapled to horizontal course seams and corner notches.

Log Jam chink bead (Tan) applied over backer rod.

Checks filled with backer rod and covered with Log Builder caulk (Woodtone).

A clear topcoat of Cascade applied last.

Interior: Logs were lightly sanded followed by a well-tooled bead of Log Builder caulk (Tan).

High Sierra (Bronze Sycamore) stain was brushed on logs and finished pine paneling.

OTHER MATERIAL

Impel Rod: At the base of all exterior stair-rail posts, an Impel Rod was inserted and plugged.

Initial Log Home Maintenance

The first six months in your new home requires a somewhat vigilant eye on air and water infiltration.

Even if you have been very careful with the initial application of the primary sealant, there are many reasons why subsequent touch-ups may be necessary. Make a note of any areas that may need attention.

Next, watch how different weather patterns affect your home. For instance:

1. What walls get the harshest sunlight?
2. What walls receive the most moisture from rain?
3. Where does snow build up around the base of the walls?

The purpose of this exercise is to anticipate where future problems may occur and decide on the appropriate remedy. This will keep your home looking newer and will require less maintenance and fewer costly repairs down the road.

The second application of the topcoat should be done sometime in the spring of the following year. You can do this yourself. If you call a professional to reapply the material, this is a perfect opportunity to address other areas of concern. Subsequent applications are determined by your answers to the three questions above.

The easiest way to tell if you need another application of topcoat is to do the following: On a reasonably overcast day, go to the wall that seems to get the harshest sunlight *and* the most rain. If that happens to be two different walls, pick a spot in the middle. With your garden hose or a cup of water, wet the wall down at eye level. Watch as the water runs off the logs, paying particular attention to the top of the logs as it runs down. If the water beads and runs off, your topcoat is still doing its job. If not, it is time to reapply.

Log home maintenance should not be a difficult task. Once you establish a pattern, it becomes easy. The important thing to remember is that your home has four potential enemies:

1. sunlight
2. moisture

3. insects

4. you

As long as you protect your home against the first two, you will effectively take care of the last two.

Moisture Content Test

Date		Species		Job	
Temp.		Type		Name	
RH		Size		Location	

Notes:

sample	s/mc	h/mc	sample	s/mc	h/mc
1			11		
2			12		
3			13		
4			14		
5			15		
6			16		
7			17		
8			18		
9			19		
10			20		
avg.			avg.		

Moisture Content Test

Date		Species		Job	
Temp.		Type		Name	
RH		Size		Location	

Notes:

sample	s/mc	h/mc	sample	s/mc	h/mc
1			11		
2			12		
3			13		
4			14		
5			15		
6			16		
7			17		
8			18		
9			19		
10			20		
avg.			avg.		

Resources

Company Resources

An * after Web addresses denotes I have used their products. A ** denotes I have not used their products, but I have information about them.

Caulks, Chinks, Stains

This list is comprised mainly of the companies I am familiar with. There are sure to be many other fine company resources I have not listed here.

Coronado Paint Company
308 Old County Rd.
Edgewater, FL 32132
(800) 883-4193
www.coronadopaint.com*

ISK Biocides, Inc.
416 E. Brooks Rd.
Memphis, TN 38109
(800) 238-2523
www.woodguard.com*

Perma-Chink Systems, Inc.
1605 Prosser Rd.
Knoxville, TN 37914
www.permachink.com*

The Sansin Corporation
3377 Egremont Dr.
Strathroy, ON N7G 3H6
Canada
www.sansin.com*

Sashco
10300 E. 107th Pl.
Brighton, CO 80601
(800) 767-5656
www.sashco.com*

Schroeder Log Home Supply, Inc.
1101 SE 7th Ave.
Grand Rapids, MN 55744
(800) 359-6614
www.loghelp.com*

Weatherall Company, Inc.
106 Industrial Way
Charlestown, IN 47111
(800) 367-7068
www.weatherall.com*

Tools, Equipment, and Other Materials

Abatron, Inc.
5501 95th Ave.
Kenosha, WI 53144
(800) 445-1754
www.abatron.com*

Albion Engineering Co.
2080A Wheatsheaf La.
Philadelphia, PA 19124-5091
(215) 535-3476
www.albioneng.com*

Clemco Industries Corp.
1 Cable Car Dr.
Washington, MO 63090
(314) 239-0300
www.clemcoindustries.com*

Delmhorst Instrument Co.
51 Indian La. East
Towaco, NJ 07082
(800) 222-0638
www.delmhorst.com*

Lee Valley Tools, Ltd.
12 E. River St.
Ogdensburg, NY 13669
(800) 871-8158
www.leevalley.com*

Northern Tool & Equipment Co.
P.O. Box 1499
Burnsville, MN 55337-0499
(800) 556-7885
www.northerntool.com*

Tool Crib of the North
www.amazon.com*
access Tools & Hardware

Woodworker's Supply, Inc.
1108 N. Glenn Rd.
Casper, WY 82601
(800) 645-9292
www.woodworker.com*

General Information Web Sites

I am always looking for reliable resources for information. Here are some sites I have visited and/or use.

www.fpl.fs.fed.us/pub_lists

The Forest Products Laboratory site. It has excellent access for numerous technical topics concerning wood.

www.fpl.fs.fed.us/tmu/publications

The Forest Products Laboratory technical marketing unit. It combines most of the titles available above with other applicable titles.

www.epa.gov/pesticides/factsheets/chemical

Site for information on chemical components of pesticides and fungicides.

www.ccohs.ca/oshanswers

Information available on chemical compounds.

www.greensmiths.com/insecticides

Information on wood boring insects.

www.alert-pest.net/cat.ofwoodboringinsects

Information on wood-boring insects.

www.rmc-construction.com/loghomes
Excellent site for discussion on log home construction considerations.

www.msue.msu.edu/msue/imp/mod02/01500631
Michigan State University Extension service site.

www.gfc.state.ga.us/publications/ruralforestry/
    loghomeconstruction.pdf
Georgia Forestry Commission site.

www.ars.usda.gov/is/fullstop
USDA site discussion on Formosan termite identification.

http://termites.tamu.edu/
Texas A&M University paper on termite species identification.

www.buildinggreen.com/features/tm/thermal.html
Building Green paper on mass enhanced R-values.

Product Information Web Sites

This is not a complete list of manufacturers of log home specific products, but I am familiar with these. A word of warning when accessing Web sites: Everyone and their products are better than everyone else. Your decision to use a specific product should be based on research into what products work best in your area.

www.alsnetbiz.com/homeimprovement/tsp (cleaners, preservatives)
www.menco.com (stains)
www.ewoodcare.com (cleaners, preservatives)
www.abrp.com/logcare (epoxy)
www.floodco.com (CWF stains)
www.prginc.com (epoxy)
www.saversystems.com (stains)
www.superdeck.com (stains)
www.thompsononline.com (clear finishes)
www.zinsser.com (Wolman finish and preservative)
www.wagnerspraytech.com (airless spray equipment)
www.wwwagner.com (moisture meters)
www.standardtar.com (Organi-clear stains)
www.olympic.com (Olympic stains)
www.cuprinol.com (Cuprinol stains)
www.penofin.com (penofin stains)
www.timbertekuv.com (Timber-Tek stains)

www.unitedcoatings.com (In-wood stains)

www.mfgsealants.com (TWP stains)

www.rhinoguard.com (Rhinoguard stains)

www.cabotstains.com (Cabot stains)

www.woodiron.com (Wood Iron stains)

Glossary

absorptive. The ability to attract moisture.

acclimate. To adapt to the regional equilibrium moisture level.

adhesion. Reference to a sealant's ability to stick to a log component base.

back brush. The act of vigorously brushing finish application into a log component.

bead. The initial and finished application appearance of sealants.

borate. Classification of a log preservative.

bound water. Moisture existing in wood fiber cell walls.

butt joints. Two or more log members adjoining one another.

catface. Deep scarring left from a live tree wound.

caustic. Reference to a type of log cleaner's corrosive cleaning ability.

cellulose. One of three primary components in wood cells.

CFM. "Cubic feet per minute" or volume of air generated at a specific PSI.

chalking. Powdery substance on the surface of an existing sealant bead. A sign of sealant breaking down at the end of its service life.

coating. Another term for *finish*, usually referring to solid color stains and/or paint.

cohesion. The ability of a sealant to maintain solidity under various stress conditions.

compatibility. The ability of a finish *and* sealant to work together regardless of which one was applied first.

component. Reference to all log members collectively.

course. Name given to log members laid horizontally in log walls.

damp wood. Log members with a moisture content in excess of 20 percent.

decay. Evidence of a condition caused by fungal or insect damage.

desorptive. The ability to shed moisture.

discoloration. Description of condition caused by weathering and/or molding.

EMC. "Equilibrium moisture content" or moisture content of log components that have acclimated.

EML. "Equilibrium moisture level" or reference to regional average moisture levels for log components to reach to acclimate.

epoxy. Material used to solidify log components suffering some form of decay. Two-part (resin and hardener), exterior use, and marine quality.

erosion. The act of wood fibers being atmospherically removed in the weathering process.

extractives. Wood chemicals leaching from heartwood onto the log surface, causing staining.

finish. General classification of liquid coverings for log components.

frass. Also *saw scat.* Insect excretions found in sawdust from boring or exit holes.

free water. Log moisture component found in cell cavities.

FSP. "Fiber saturation point" or the point at which free water has evaporated from cell cavities, leaving bound water in cell walls.

fungi. Type of rot found in damp wood.

fuzzing. Texture left on a log surface from a cleaning application.

green wood. Term for log material with a moisture content of 20 percent or greater.

growth rings. Annual addition of wood cells formed during the growth process. Two subclassifications include *earlywood* and *latewood.*

heartwood. The innermost component of a log member. Also the most stable component when describing *absorptive* and *desorptive* characteristics.

humidity. Reference to an atmospheric condition. Described in *absolute* and *relative* terms.

KD/AD. "Kiln dried/air dried" or method of process for bringing log components to the level of moisture content existing at a certain point.

lap joints. Description of overlapping seams in a finish application.

leaching. Process of moisture migrating toward the surface of a log member.

lignin. One of three components in wood fibers.

longitudinal. Direction reference to shrinkage values.

mass enhanced R-value. The appropriate measure of thermal efficiency of log homes.

MC. "Moisture content" or percent of moisture found in a log member.

members. Reference to specific log materials.

moisture. Existence of water or humidity as it relates to a condition.

mold/mildew. Name or classification of moisture attracting spores. Usually the first sign of a rot or decay condition.

oil-based. Description of type of finish. Oil-based finishes are usually penetrating finishes.

oil-borne. Description of the carrying agent for a finish application. Solvent cleanup.

outgassing. A condition caused by the puncturing of *closed cell* backer rod.

penetrating. Description of the ability of a finish to permeate the log surface.

pot life. The amount of time to work an epoxy blend before it starts to cure.

preservative. A term given to classify certain chemicals possessing VOC's (volatile organic compounds).

profile. General classification of the description of log surfaces.

PSI. "Pounds per square inch" or the value of pressure generated by an air compressor.

radial. Direction reference to shrinkage values. Measurement is from the heart to the radius of the log member.

reaction wood. General description of irregular growth patterns found in all wood species.

repair. A term for describing remedial work that fixes a problem without reference to historical conditions.

repellent. General description for water excluding applications that do not possess preservative compounds.

restore. A term for describing remedial work with reference to historical conditions.

sapwood. The outer component of a log member after debarking. It possesses the most *absorptive* and *desorptive* capabilities of the log components.

scar. A term for the appearance of the location of healed wood material.

scat. Also *frass*. Insect excretions found in sawdust from boring or exit holes.

sealant. General classification of material used to seal log components.

seams. A reference to the joint between log members.

semitransparent. General classification of finishes possessing certain amounts of solid materials that provide protection against the damaging UV rays of sunlight.

settling. A term for overall log movement as the components are acclimating to EML.

settling gaps. Spaces left between log components and other construction to allow for shrinkage and settling.

settling plates. Devices used to manually adjust log posts during the acclimation phase.

shelf life. The amount of time a particular sealant or finish can sit unused in its original, unopened container.

shrink/swell. The process of seasonal log movement affected by humidity levels. Expressed as an expected percent.

shrinkage. A term given to the amount an individual log member will reduce in size during the acclimation phase. Expressed as a percentage.

slip joints. A term given to the slot cut in dimension materials attached to log components to allow for settling during the acclimation phase *and* shrinking/swelling over the life of the structure.

solid color. A term for the final appearance of finish material on a log surface. Generally nonpenetrating.

solvent. A material for thinning or cleaning, such as denatured alcohol, paint thinner, and mineral spirits.

splash back. Condition caused on the lower section of a log wall by rainfall splashing dirt on the log surface.

substrate. Structure existing under the surface or applied material. Reference is to its condition.

sunlight. Reference to harmful ultraviolet rays in the weathering process.

tangential. Direction reference to shrinkage values. Measurement is from surface to surface or across the grain of the wood material.

tooling. Process of smoothing the initial applied sealant bead to the final appearance.

toxicity. A term or description of a particular material's chemical properties causing some form of adverse reaction to other living beings.

transparent. General classification of finishes with no solid materials to provide protection from harmful ultraviolet rays.

two-point adhesion. Description of the ideal bonding properties of sealants to wood substrate.

water-based. A type of finish. Water-based finishes are usually nonpenetrating.

water-borne. Description of a carrying agent for the finish application. Soap and water cleanup.

WR. "Water repellent" or general classification of finishes possessing some form of water repellent property.

WRP. "Water repellent preservative" or general classification of finishes possessing some form of water repellent *and* a preservative.

Bibliography

Blast Off 2. Second edition. Clemco Industries Corp., 1994.

Ken Collier, "Bug Control," *Family Handyman,* April 1996.

Encyclopedia of Wood. Revised edition. New York: Sterling Publishing, 1989.

Forbes, Reginald D. *Forestry Handbook.* Society of American Foresters. New York: Ronald Press, 1955.

Goodall, Harrison. *Log Structures, Preservation and Problem Solving.* Nashville, Tenn.: American Association of State and Local History, 1980. Out of print.

Hoadley, R. Bruce. *Understanding Wood: A Craftsman's Guide to Wood Technology.* Newtown, Conn.: Taunton Press, 2000.

Olkowski, William, et al. *Common-Sense Pest Control.* U.S. Department of Agriculture, Forest Service, Forest Products Laboratory, Newtown, Conn.: Taunton Press, 1991.

Renfroe, Jim, et al. *The Log Home Owner's Manual: A Guide to Protecting and Restoring Exterior Wood.* Advantage Entertainment, Inc. 1995.

Smulski, Stephen. *Detailing for Wood Shrinkage.* Shutesburg, Mass.: Wood Science Specialists, Inc., 1996.

White, Richard E., et al. *A Field Guide to Insects.* New York: Houghton Mifflin Company, 1970.

Williams, R. Sam. *Selection and Application of Exterior Stains for Wood.* FPL-GTR-106. U.S. Department of Agriculture, Forest Service, Forest Products Laboratory, 1999.

Williams, R. Sam. *Water Repellents and Water Repellent Preservatives for Wood.* FPL-GTR-109. U.S. Department of Agriculture, Forest Service, Forest Products Laboratory, 1999.

The Wood Handbook: Wood as an Engineering Material. FPL-GTR-113. U.S. Department of Agriculture, Forest Service, Forest Products Laboratory, 1999.

Kersten, Philip J. *Wood Preservation in the 90's and Beyond.* Forest Products Society, Proceedings No. 7308, Madison, Wis., 1994.

INDEX